Magdalena Ozorowska *Grammar explanations*
Andrea Schwingshackl *Vocabulary / Cultural studies*

A 1.2

MENSCHEN

Deutsch als Fremdsprache
Glossary XXL

Deutsch – Englisch
German – English

Hueber Verlag

5.   4.   3.   Die letzten Ziffern
2021   20   19   18   17   bezeichnen Zahl und Jahr des Druckes.
Alle Drucke dieser Auflage können, da unverändert,
nebeneinander benutzt werden.
1. Auflage
© 2014 Hueber Verlag GmbH & Co. KG, München, Deutschland
Umschlaggestaltung: Sieveking · Agentur für Kommunikation, München
Zeichnungen: Michael Mantel, Barum
Layout: Sieveking · Agentur für Kommunikation, München
Satz: Sieveking · Agentur für Kommunikation, München
Druck und Bindung: Firmengruppe APPL, aprinta druck GmbH, Wemding
Printed in Germany
ISBN 978–3–19–061901–6

Art. 530_12986_001_03

Deutsche welle / kurse
langsam gesprochene

Contents

Lektion 13: Wir suchen das Hotel Maritim.

1

ab·biegen	Nach 600 Metern bitte rechts abbiegen.	to turn (left/right/off)
an·machen	Die Frau macht den Navigator an.	to turn on, to switch on
im (lokal)	Die beiden sitzen im Auto.	in (local)
fahren	Fahr weiter.	to drive
geradeaus	Fahr geradeaus.	straight ahead
der Kilometer, -	1000 Meter sind ein Kilometer.	kilometer
links	Bitte links abbiegen.	left
der Navigator, Navigatoren	*Die Frau macht den Navigator an.*	navigator
rechts	Fahren Sie nach rechts.	right
der Stadtplan, ⸚e	Der Stadtplan ist nicht falsch.	city map
stimmen	Mein Stadtplan stimmt.	here: to be correct
wenden	*Bitte wenden Sie.*	to turn, to reverse
weiter·fahren	Fahr geradeaus weiter.	to drive/carry on
zurück·fahren	Fahr zurück.	to drive back

> **TIPP** What is the best way to memorize new words?
> Think of tricks that help to remember vocabulary.

Links oder rechts?
Das ist ganz einfach.
L wie links.

BILDLEXIKON

auf	Der Stab ist auf dem Würfel.	on top of
an	Der Stab ist an dem Würfel.	at, by
hinter	Der Stab ist hinter dem Würfel.	behind
in	Der Stab ist in dem Würfel.	inside
neben	Der Stab ist neben dem Würfel.	next to
über	Der Stab ist über der Pyramide.	above
unter	Der Stab ist unter der Pyramide.	under
vor	Der Stab ist vor dem Würfel.	in front of
zwischen	Der Stab ist zwischen den Würfeln.	in between

2

der Blick, -e	Der Blick von oben: Was sehen Sie?	view
der Stab, ⸚e	*Wo ist der Stab?*	rod, wand, pole, stick
der Würfel, -	*Der Stab ist hinter dem Würfel.*	cube

3

die Polizei (Sg.)	Wo ist die Polizei?	police (pl.)
die Post (Sg.)	Ich suche die Post.	post office

die Stadtmitte, -n	Das Hotel ist in der Stadtmitte.	centre of town
das Zentrum, Zentren	die Stadtmitte = das Zentrum	centre

4

die Nähe:	Das Hotel ist in der Nähe.	proximity, vicinity:
in der Nähe von		nearby, close to

5

am (lokal)	Die Post ist am Bahnhof.	by (local)
durch·kommen	Sie kommen unter einer Brücke durch.	to come through
ein·tragen	*Tragen Sie den Weg in den Plan ein.*	*to register, to record*
der Plan, ̈e	Tragen Sie den Weg in den Plan ein.	plan, map
vorbei·fahren	Fahren Sie an den Cafés vorbei.	to ride past
das Haus, ̈e r	An den Häusern fahren Sie auch vorbei.	house

6

✓ bauen	„Bauen" Sie Bilder.	to build

7

fremd	Ich bin auch fremd hier.	foreign
trotzdem	Trotzdem: Dankeschön.	nonetheless, regardless

8

das Gedächtnis, -se	*Wie gut ist Ihr Gedächtnis?*	*memory*

9

der Moment, -e	Haben Sie einen Moment Zeit?	moment
nun	Bitten Sie nun höflich um Hilfe.	now, at the moment

jdn um Hilfe bitten: ask sb. for help.

LERNZIELE

die Ampel, -n	An der Ampel fahren Sie nach links.	traffic light
der Dativ, -e	*Dativ: vor dem Restaurant*	*dative case*
die Institution, -en	*Institutionen wie Bank, Post ...*	*institution*
lokal	*lokale Präpositionen vor, in an ...*	*local*
nach (lokal)	Fahren Sie nach links.	to, towards
der Platz, ̈e	Plätze in der Stadt	square, place
vor (lokal)	Wo? – Vor dem Restaurant.	in front of (local)
die Wegbeschreibung, -en	*Machen Sie eine Wegbeschreibung.*	*direction (instructions on how to reach a destination)*

bei: jdm Hilfen suchen: to seek sb's help.

Lektion 14: Wie findest du Ottos Haus?

1

das Computerspiel, -e	Spielen Sie gern Computerspiele?	computer game

BILDLEXIKON

der Balkon, -e und -s	Da oben ist sein Balkon.	balcony
der Baum, ̈e	Im Garten steht ein Baum.	tree
die Blume, -n	Im Garten sind viele Blumen.	flower
das Erdgeschoss, -e (EG)	Im Erdgeschoss sind die Küche und das Wohnzimmer.	ground floor, first floor
die Garage, -n	Da hinten ist die Garage.	garage
der Keller, -	Hat das Haus auch einen Keller?	basement, cellar
der Stock, ̈e: erster Stock	Im ersten Stock sind die Schlafzimmer.	floor, level

3

das Arbeitszimmer, -	Wo ist sein Arbeitszimmer?	study, home office
das Bad, ̈er	Das Bad ist im ersten Stock.	bathroom
der Flur, -e	Du stehst im Flur. Links ist die Toilette.	hallway, corridor
das Kinderzimmer, -	Die Wohnung hat zwei Kinderzimmer.	nursery, children's room
die Küche, -n	Die Küche ist klein.	kitchen
das Schlafzimmer, -	Das Schlafzimmer ist aber groß.	bedroom
die Toilette, -n	Entschuldigung, wo ist die Toilette, bitte?	toilet
das Wohnzimmer, -	Das Wohnzimmer ist neben der Küche.	living room

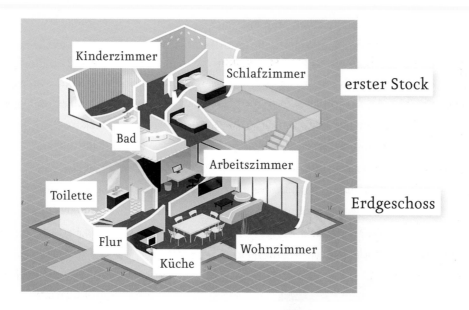

ZIMMER IM HAUS

5

hinten	Da hinten ist Ottos Garage.	back, behind
mögen	Seinen Garten mag ich nicht so.	to like
oben	Da oben ist sein Balkon.	above, up there
sein/seine (Possessiv-artikel)	Das ist Otto. Und das ist seine Nachbarin Vanilla.	his (possessive pronoun of *er* and *es*)
unten	Wo ist der Garten? – Da unten.	below, down, at the bottom
vorn	Wo ist das Arbeitszimmer? – Da vorn.	at the front

6

aus·sehen	Dein Garten sieht toll aus.	to look
nicht so: nicht so gut	Vanillas Haus finde ich nicht so gut.	not so: not so good

8

das Apartment, -s	Apartment mit 32 m²	apartment, flat
bezahlen	Man bezahlt die Miete jeden Monat.	to pay
dringend	Polizistin sucht dringend Wohnung.	urgent
der Herd, -e	In der Küche stehen der Kühlschrank und der Herd.	cooker, stove
inkl (inklusive)	Sind die Nebenkosten inklusive?	inclusive
der Kontakt, -e	Kontakt: vanilla@btx.net	contact
der Kühlschrank, ⸚e	Ist die Küche mit Kühlschrank und Herd?	fridge
leer	Die neue Wohnung ist nicht leer.	empty
die Miete, -n	Was kostet die Miete?	rent
mitten	Wohnen wie auf dem Land und doch mitten in der Stadt!	amidst, in the middle of
möbliert	Die Wohnung ist möbliert.	furnished
die Monatsmiete, -n	Die Monatsmiete ist 320 Euro.	monthly rent
der Müll (Sg.)	Die Nebenkosten sind für Wasser, Müll und Licht.	rubbish, garbage
die Nebenkosten (NK) (Pl.)	320 € inkl. NK	utilities, additional costs
plus	Die Miete ist 880 Euro plus Nebenkosten.	plus
die Polizistin, -nen	Die Polizistin sucht eine Wohnung.	police woman
der Quadratmeter, -	Wie viel Quadratmeter hat die Wohnung?	square meter
der Schlafraum, ⸚e	Das Apartment hat einen Wohn- und Schlafraum.	bedroom
der Stellplatz, ⸚e	ein Stellplatz für das Auto	parking space
die Tiefgarage, -n	Das Haus hat eine Tiefgarage.	underground car park
der Vermieter, -	Der Vermieter bekommt die Miete.	landlord
die Warmmiete, -n	Die Warmmiete ist inklusive Warmwasser.	rent including heating, all-in bill
der Wohnraum, ⸚e	Das Apartment hat nur einen Wohnraum.	living space/area
die Wohnung, -en	Wer bietet eine Wohnung an?	flat

der Wohnungsmarkt, ⸚e	Lesen Sie die Anzeigen im Wohnungsmarkt.	housing market
z.B. (zum Beispiel)	Man bezahlt Nebenkosten, zum Beispiel für Wasser und Müll.	for example (eg.)
die 2-Zimmer-Wohnung, -en	Ich suche eine 2-Zimmer-Wohnung.	two-room apartment

notice
report, announcements

> **TIPP** Describe words.
>
> Hier kann man kochen. → Küche
> Das bezahle ich für meine Wohnung. → Miete

9

✓ das Bauernhaus, ⸚er	Mein Traumhaus ist ein altes Bauernhaus.	farm house
die Fabrik, -en	Ich wohne in einer Fabrik.	factory
der Fluss, ⸚e	Neben dem Haus gibt es einen Fluss.	river
der Freizeitpark, -s	Vor dem Haus ist ein Freizeitpark.	leisure park, theme park
✓ der Fußballplatz, ⸚e	Hinter dem Haus gibt es einen Fußballplatz.	football pitch
✓ der Leuchtturm, ⸚e	Mein Haus ist ein Leuchtturm.	lighthouse
✓ der Stall, ⸚e	Neben dem Haus steht ein Stall.	stable
der Swimmingpool, -s	Im Garten ist ein Swimmingpool.	swimming pool
das Traumhaus, ⸚er	Wie sieht Ihr Traumhaus aus?	dream house/home
✓ der Wald, ⸚er	Hinter dem Haus ist ein Wald.	forest
✓ das Zelt, -e	Ich wohne in einem Zelt.	tent

10

negativ	Ihre neue Wohnung: Was ist negativ?	negative
positiv	Positiv ist: Das Bad hat ein Fenster.	positive
um·ziehen	Ich bin umgezogen.	to move (home)

LERNZIELE

der Eigenname, -n	Eigennamen: Otto, Vanilla …	personal name
der Genitiv, -e	Genitiv bei Eigennamen: Ottos Haus, Vanillas Haus	genitive case
die Wohnungs-anzeige, -n	Lesen Sie die Wohnungsanzeigen.	advert for a flat

Lektion 15: In Giesing wohnt das Leben!

2

der Hafen, ⸚	Ich sehe den Hafen.	harbour, port
das Meer, -e	Ich sehe das Meer, ich mag den Blick.	sea, ocean

BILDLEXIKON

die Altstadt, ⸚e	Die Altstadt von Zürich ist schön.	old town
die Bibliothek, -en	Gibt einen Link zur Bibliothek?	library

das Geschäft, -e	Ich suche ein Geschäft für Souvenirs.	shop
die Jugendherberge, -n	Gibt es hier eine Jugendherberge?	youth hostel
der Kindergarten, ¨	Zum Kindergarten ist es nicht weit.	nursery
die Kirche, -n	Gibt es eine Kirche in der Nähe?	church
der Laden, ¨	Es gibt viele Läden in dem Viertel.	shop
der Markt, ¨e	Der Markt ist jeden Donnerstag.	market
das Rathaus, ¨er	Wo ist das Rathaus? – Im Zentrum.	town hall
das Schloss, ¨er	Wie heißt das Schloss?	castle
der Spielplatz, ¨e	Die Kinder spielen auf dem Spielplatz.	playground
der Turm, ¨e	Ein Leuchtturm ist ein Turm.	tower

das Schloss, ¨er   der Spielplatz, ¨e   die Kirche, -n   der Hafen, ¨   das Meer, -e   der Park, -s   der Turm, ¨e   der Markt(platz), ¨e

---

TIPP Look at the vocabulary in the chapter *In der Stadt*. Close your book and try to write down all the words with article. How many can you remember?

der Turm, der Park ...

4

aktuell	Aktuelles: Der neue Film von Sam Jung läuft jetzt im Kino.	current, up-to-date
der Arbeiter, -	Hier leben Arbeiter und Studenten.	worker
der Ausländer, -	In Giesing leben Deutsche und Ausländer gut zusammen.	foreign national
danken	Ich danke dir.	to thank so (for sth.)
davon	*Was davon gibt es auch in Ihrer Stadt?*	*of them, therefrom*
der/die Deutsche, -n	Wohnen dort viele Deutsche?	male/female person from Germany
die Ecke, -n: um die Ecke	Der Kindergarten ist gleich um die Ecke.	corner: around the corner
die Fanseite, -n	*Für alle Glückstadt-Spieler gibt es eine Fanseite.*	*fan page*
gehören	Der Stadtteil gehört uns allen.	to belong to
gratulieren	Hallo Marlene! Gratuliere! Dein Blog gefällt mir.	to congratulate
der Heimatort, -e	Gibt es in Ihrem Heimatort viele Läden?	home town
helfen	Dein Text über Giesing hilft mir.	to help

hin·kommen	Wir kommen gut zu Fuß hin.	to get to a place
in: in sein	Giesing ist nicht in. Giesing ist normal.	something quite in fashion, to be flavour of the month
das Kochrezept, -e	neue Kochrezepte auf www.kochnetz.net	cooking recipe
die Landschaft, -en	Ich liebe diese Landschaft.	landscape
das Lieblingsviertel, -	Was ist Ihr Lieblingsviertel?	favourite neighbourhood
mir	Dein Text hilft mir.	me (personal pronoun, dative)
das Nachbarhaus, ⸚er	Der Friseur ist gleich im Nachbarhaus.	neighbouring house, house next door
nämlich	Marlenes Text über Giesing hilft mir. Ich möchte nämlich bald in München studieren.	namely, that is to say
der Regen, - (Sg.)	Regen oder Sonne?	rain
das Reisebüro, -s	Wie heißt das Reisebüro um die Ecke?	travel agency
die Ruhe (Sg.)	Marlene liebt die Ruhe auf dem Land.	silence, tranquility, serenity
schon (Modalpartikel)	Giesing ist schon okay.	modal particle, does not translate literally, may be used affirmatively (used mainly in spoken language)
die Sonne, -n	Wie ist das Wetter? Sonne?	sun
der Spieler, -	aktuelle Informationen für alle Glückstadt-Spieler	player
die Stadtteil-Biblio-thek, -en	In München gibt es Stadtteil-Bibliotheken.	library in a specific district of town
das Stadtviertel, -	Was gibt es in Ihrem Stadtviertel?	district, quarter
überall	Von hier aus kommen wir überall hin.	everywhere
das Viertel, - (Stadtviertel)	Marlene liebt ihr Viertel.	quarter
weit	Wie weit ist es bis zum Bahnhof?	here: far
die Werkstatt, ⸚en	Hier sind auch viele Werkstätten.	workshop, factory
das Wetter (Sg.)	Das Wetter in München ist super.	weather

5

der Berg, -e	Saskia gefallen die Berge.	mountain
euch	Gefällt euch das?	you (all) (accusative and dative 2nd pers. pl.)
ihm	Das Haus gehört Otto. = Es gehört ihm.	his (dative 3rd pers. sing.)
ihnen	Wie gefällt es ihnen in München?	them (dative, 3rd pers. pl.)
(das) Kanada	Ich mache oft in Kanada Urlaub.	Canada
der Urlaubsort, -e	Wem gefällt der Urlaubsort?	holiday destination

LERNZIELE

eigentlich	Gibt es eigentlich ein Kino in Giesing?	actually
die Einrichtung (Sg.)	Einrichtungen und Orte in der Stadt	here: facility
normal	Giesing ist ganz normal.	normal

MODUL-PLUS LESEMAGAZIN

1

bayerisch	Magst du bayerische Blasmusik?	Bavarian
beliebt	Der Biergarten ist bei Touristen sehr beliebt.	popular
der Biergarten, ⁼	Der Biergarten am Seehaus ist sehr schön.	beer garden
die Blasmusik (Sg.)	Im Turm spielt eine bayerische Blasmusik für die Gäste.	brass music
der/die Einheimische, -n	Einheimische und Touristen mögen den Biergarten.	local, native (people)
der Englische Garten	Der Englische Garten ist mehr als 200 Jahre alt.	"English Garden" (a large public park in the centre of Munich)
die Fläche, -n	Der Park hat mehr als vier Quadratkilometer Fläche.	area
die Freundschaft, -en	Das Teehaus ist ein Zeichen für die Freundschaft von München und Sapporo.	friendship, amity
griechisch	Der Monopteros ist ein griechischer Tempel.	Greek
die Großstadt, ⁼e	München ist eine Großstadt.	city
grün: im Grünen	Nur 800 Meter und schon ist man im Grünen.	in the countryside
der Hügel, -	Der Monopteros ist auf einem Hügel.	hill
das Jahrhundert, -e	Im 18. Jahrhundert war ein Park noch etwas Besonderes.	century
der Lieblingspark, -s	Haben Sie einen Lieblingspark?	favourite park
die Olympiastadt, ⁼e	München und Sapporo sind Olympiastädte.	Olympic city
das Prozent, -e	Wir haben noch nicht einmal 30 Prozent vom Park gesehen.	percent
der Quadratkilometer, -	Ein Park mit mehr als vier Quadratkilometern – das ist sehr viel.	square kilometer
die Richtung, -en	Jetzt gehen wir etwa 800 Meter in Richtung Stadtmitte.	direction
der Sitzplatz, ⁼e	Der Biergarten hat 7.000 Sitzplätze.	seat
die Städtepartnerschaft, -en	München hat eine Städtepartnerschaft mit Sapporo.	town twinning, sister-city arrangement
das Stadtzentrum, Stadtzentren	Vom Stadtzentrum sind es nur etwa 800 Meter zum Englischen Garten.	centre of town
starten	Ich starte meinen Spaziergang woanders.	to begin, to start
die Station, -en	Ich fahre vier Stationen.	station
der Tempel, -	Der Monopteros ist ein Tempel.	temple
üblich	Volksnähe war im 18. Jahrhundert nicht üblich.	usual, common

die Volksnähe (Sg.)	Volksnähe war im 18. Jahrhundert nicht üblich.	to be down to earth, in touch with people
woanders	Ich beginne den Spaziergang woanders.	elsewhere
das Zeichen, -	Das Teehaus ist eine Zeichen für die Freundschaft von München und Sapporo.	sign

MODUL-PLUS FILM-STATIONEN

1

der Lieblingsplatz, ¨e	Was ist Ihr Lieblingsplatz?	favourite place

2

die Superwohnung, -en	Das ist eine Superwohnung.	super flat, amazing flat

3

der Bär, -en	Im Berner Wappen sieht man einen Bären.	bear
der Einwohner, -	Wie viele Einwohner hat die Stadt?	resident, inhabitant
das Hochdeutsch (Sg.)	Sprechen Sie Hochdeutsch?	High German, standard German
das Wappen, -	Im Berner Wappen sieht man einen Bären.	crest, emblem

MODUL-PLUS PROJEKT LANDESKUNDE

1

die Atmosphäre, -n	Besonders gern mag ich die Atmosphäre am Hafen.	atmosphere
das Containerschiff, -e	Spannend ist der Hafen mit den Containerschiffen.	container ship
die Elbe	Hamburg liegt an der Elbe.	Elbe (river in the north of Germany)
elektronisch	Dort gibt es auch elektronische Produkte.	electronic
das Gewürz, -e	In der Speicherstadt lagern Waren von den Schiffen, z.B. Gewürze.	spice
irgendwann	Vielleicht sehen wir uns irgendwann mal?	sometime
der Kakao, -s	Kakao, Kaffee, Tee, Gewürze – Waren von den Containerschiffen	cocoa
der Kirchturm, ¨e	Der Blick vom Kirchturm ist toll.	church steeple/tower
die Kultur, -en	Hamburg ist eine Kulturstadt.	culture
kulturell	In der Speicherstadt gibt es viele kulturelle Veranstaltungen.	cultural
die Kunst, ¨e	In Hamburg gibt es alles: Kunst und Kultur, Restaurants und Bars …	art
lagern	In der Speicherstadt lagern Waren.	to store
die Lesung, -en	Es gibt auch Lesungen und Theateraufführungen.	reading
die Lieblingsstadt, ¨e	Meine Lieblingsstadt ist Hamburg.	favourite city

das Schiff, -e	Im Hafen liegen viele Schiffe.	ship
spannend	Der Hafen ist besonders spannend.	exciting
die Speicherstadt, ⸚e	Auch die Speicherstadt ist sehr interessant.	warehouse district (in Hamburg)
die Theateraufführung, -en	Hast du die Theateraufführung gesehen?	theatre play
das Wahrzeichen, -	Die Kirche St. Michaelis ist das Wahrzeichen von Hamburg.	landmark

MODUL-PLUS AUSKLANG

1

der Tanzschritt, -e	Lernen Sie die Tanzschritte.	dance-step

2

ach!	Ach, mein Schatz, ich finde es super in Berlin.	Alas!, oh!
betonen	Betonen Sie, was Ihnen gefällt und was nicht.	to emphasize, to accentuate
entscheiden	Entscheiden Sie: Wo sind Sie lieber?	to decide
hin·fahren	Da fahren wir jetzt hin.	to travel to
das Schnucki, -s	Und du, Schnucki? Findest du es auch so schön hier?	darling, sweetie pie

Grammar Explanations

Lektion 13: Wir suchen das Hotel Maritim.

Dative case

The **dative case** is the third German case. The dative ending of the article is **-em** for masculine and neuter, and **-er** for feminine nouns. In plural most nouns also add an **-n** to their form, unless they end in -s or already in -n.

	nominative	dative
masculine	der / ein Bahnhof	**dem** / ein**em** Bahnhof
neutral	das / ein Hotel	**dem** / ein**em** Hotel
feminine	die / eine Ampel	**der** / ein**er** Ampel
plural	die / — Häuser	**den** / — Häuser**n**

This case is used for **indirect objects** and for the **object of specific verbs** but it is also used for the **object of some prepositions**, e.g.:

Das Hotel ist **neben dem** Bahnhof.   *The hotel is **next to the** train station.*

Local prepositions with dative case

Some prepositions will be followed by the dative case, if the phrase can answer the question **wo?** (where?):

auf (*on, on top of sth.*) Das Buch liegt **auf dem** Tisch.   *The book is lying on the table.*

an (*at, on*) Der Mann wartet **an der** Ampel.   *The man is waiting at the traffic light.*

in (*in, inside*) Das Café ist **in der** Stadtmitte.   *The cafe is in the city centre.*

neben (*next to*) Die Bank ist **neben der** Post.   *The bank is next to the post office.*

hinter (*behind, in the back of*) Der Parkplatz ist **hinter dem** Hotel.   *The parking is in the back of the hotel.*

vor (*in front of*) Mein Auto ist **vor dem** Haus.   *My car is in front of the house.*

unter (*under, beneath*) Der Mann steht **unter der** Brücke.   *The man is standing under the bridge.*

über (*above, over, across*) Der Kalender hängt **über dem** Bett.   *The calendar is hanging above the bed.*

zwischen (*between → either two nouns in dative case or a noun in plural dative form are required!*) Die Kirche ist **zwischen dem** Park und **dem** Marktplatz.   *The church is between the park and the market place.*

Grammar Explanations

Contraction of preposition and definite article

Some of the prepositions will contract with the definite article in dative case, e.g.:

in + de**m** → **im**:   Das Café ist **im** Stadtzentrum.
an + de**m** → **am**:   Ich sitze **am** Tisch.

Irregular verb helfen

The verb **helfen** (*to help*) is irregular and has a vowel change **e → i**.

		helfen
singular	ich	helfe
	du	hilfst
	er/sie	hilft
plural	wir	helfen
	ihr	helft
	sie/Sie	helfen

Ich **helfe** Peter und du **hilfst** Anna.   *I am helping Peter and you are helping Anna.*

Ordinal numbers and giving directions

Ordinal numbers are useful for giving directions, for example: *the first, the second, the third street on the left...*

erste – *first*
Gehen Sie **die erste** Straße links.   *Turn into the first street on the left.*

zweite – *second*
Fahren Sie **die zweite** Straße rechts.   *Turn into the second street on the right.*

dritte – *third*
Die dritte Straße links ist die Schillerstraße.   *The third street on the left is the Schiller Street.*

The ordinal number takes the article of the noun:

die erste Straße rechts   *the first street on the left*
das zweite Restaurant links   *the second restaurant on the left*
der dritte Parkplatz rechts   *the third parking on the right*

Grammar Explanations

Lektion 14: Wie findest du Ottos Haus?

Possessive pronouns sein and ihr in nominative and accusative case

Possessive pronouns change according to the noun's gender, number and case. Feminine words and all plural forms have an ending **-e**, masculine nouns in accusative case have an ending **-en**.

Das ist Otto und **sein** Garten.
Ich mag **seinen** Garten nicht so.

*This is Otto and **his** garden.*
*I don't like **his** garden so much.*

Das ist Vanilla und **ihr** Haus.
Ich finde **ihr** Haus sehr gemütlich.

*This is Vanilla and **her** house.*
I find her house very cosy.

	nominative	accusative
	Da ist...	*Ich mag...*
● Garten	sein / ihr Garten	sein**en** / ihr**en** Garten
● Haus	sein / ihr Haus	sein / ihr Haus
● Küche	seine / ihre Küche	seine / ihre Küche
	Da sind...	*Ich mag...*
● Kinder	seine / ihre Kinder	seine / ihre Kinder

The genitive case with names

The genitive case shows possession. It is expressed in English by an apostrophe and the letter -s. In German, the letter **-s** is added to the name but **without an apostrophe**.

Otto**s** Haus
Maria**s** Nachbarin

Otto's house
Maria's female neighbour

The preposition von as an alternative option for the genitive case

Another way to show possession is using the preposition **of** in English or **von** in German. It is not considered more formal as the -s.

Ein Freund **von** Otto
Eine Nachbarin **von** Maria

*a friend **of** Otto's*
*a female neighbour **of** Maria's*

Ordinal numbers and locating the floor

Ordinal numbers are useful to describe the location of the flat or the floor. For the ground floor there is no number needed.

Hier ist das Erdgeschoss.	*Here is the ground floor.*
Meine Eltern wohnen im Erdgeschoss.	*My parents live on the ground floor.*

Hier ist der **erste / zweite / dritte** Stock.	*Here is the first / second / third floor.*
Ich wohne **im ersten / zweiten / dritten** Stock.	*I live on the first / second / third floor.*

Accusative case and time information

Accusative case is not only used to show the direct object in a sentence. Another function is to indicate time and frequency in phrases like:

jed**en** Monat	*every month*
nächst**en** Monat	*next month*

Max bezahlt seine Miete **jeden Monat.**	*Max pays his rent **every** month.*
Ich ziehe **nächsten Monat** um.	*I am moving house **next** month.*

Lektion 15: In Giesing wohnt das Leben!

Verbs with dative case

The dative case can be used for direct **object of specific verbs**. The best way to learn is to memorize them.

danken – to thank
Ich danke **dem Professor.** Ich danke **ihm** jetzt.   *I thank **the professor.** I thank **him** now.*

helfen – to help
Er hilft **der Lehrerin.** Er hilft **ihr** oft.   He is helping **the teacher.** He helps **her** often.

gefallen – to please, to like
Die Stadt gefällt **uns.**   *The city "pleases **us**". (We like the city)*

gehören – to belong
Das Auto gehört **dem Mann** und *The car belongs to **the man** and
der Frau dort. Das Auto gehört   **the woman** over there. The car belongs to
ihnen seit gestern.   **them** since yesterday.*

Personal pronoun in dative case

The nouns in the dative case can be replaced by pronouns.

Er hilft **mir**, aber das gefällt **ihm** nicht.   *He helps **me**, but it doesn't please **him**.*

Grammar Explanations

	personal pronoun					
nominative	ich	du	er/es/sie	wir	ihr	sie/Sie
dative	mir	dir	ihm/ihm/ihr	uns	euch	ihnen/Ihnen

To remember the personal pronouns **ihm** and **ihr**, it is very helpful to recall their English equivalents: **him = ihm, her = ihr**.

The same endings, the same lengh and even a little bit similar pronounciation.

The phrase Es gibt ...

Es gibt... is one of the most useful phrases in German. It means "there is" and "there are" in the same time, but also "it exists". The only thing to remember is, to add an object in **accusative** case to the phrase.

Gibt es hier in der Nähe **einen Laden**?	*Is there any shop nearby?*
Ja, **es gibt** hier links **einen Laden**.	*Yes, there is a shop on the left.*

Word forming with Lieblings-

The word **Lieblings**... added in front of a noun is used to talk about favourite things or people:

Mein **Lieblingsviertel** in München ist Giesing.	*My **favourite area** in Munich is Giesing.*
Meine **Lieblingssängerin** ist Christina Stürmer.	*My **favourite female singer** is Christina Stürmer.*

Why Germans like to rent their homes

Traditionally, Germans have been known as a nation of tenants rather than homeowners. Whilst many other nationalities such as the Brits are desperate to get on the property ladder, renting a home is the norm in Germany. One major reason why homeownership is not the ultimate goal for Germans is due to the absence of a housing boom which many other European countries experienced over the last decade and as a consequence the risk of long-term falling housing prices was too high. Also, a property transfer tax (*Grunderwerbssteuer*), an annual land tax (*Grundsteuer*) and a high mortgage deposit being required makes renting a more attractive option for many. Furthermore, high quality rental accommodation is available in Germany and since tenants generally rent long term, properties are well looked after and kept in good condition. It is very common for owners to freshly renovate a home before new tenants move in and tenants must repaint a property before they leave.

der Grunderwerb: acquisition of land.

However, more recent surveys suggest there is an increased shift towards homeownership in Germany. Rental prices are rising steadily, competitively priced mortgages are available and interest rates have fallen slightly. As a result, more people are keen to own their own home. Another potential attraction for home buyers is the fact that housing prices are rising and therefore the risk of capital loss on property is declining. Many believe that Germany is on the brink of a property boom as seen in other European countries in the last decade.

Nonetheless, the European nation with the highest proportion of tenants is Switzerland where approximately 70% of Swiss do not own their own home. This large volume of tenants causes huge competition on the Swiss rental market making it especially difficult to find affordable accommodation in larger cities.

Useful abbreviations in real estate adverts

In order to understand the real estate advertisements, it is necessary to get familiar with the abbreviations used in this type of advert:

m² – der Quadratmeter = *square meter*
NK – die Nebenkosten = *housing costs in addition to the rent*
Zi. – das Zimmer = *room*
EG – das Erdgeschoss = *ground floor*
ca. – circa = *about, around, approx.*
inkl. – inklusive = *inclusive*

Cultural Studies

Jugendherbergen — an Idea 'Made in Germany'

A German teacher called Richard Schirrmann, who during a day out with his students got caught up in a flash rainstorm and sought shelter in an empty local school, was the inventor of youth hostels. The idea of using vacant schools as guest houses was born and this concept changed the world of travelling forever.

The first permanent youth hostel was established in 1912 in Castle Altena in the small town of Altena in western Germany, and even nowadays it is still used as such – which certainly makes an impressive location for low-cost accommodation (*Jugendherberge Burg Altena*). Schirrmann's initial idea was to provide affordable accommodation for young people from cities giving them the opportunity to enjoy fresh air and time in the country-side without breaking the budget.

Soon, the idea spread out across the globe; nowadays in Germany alone, there are more than 550 youth hostels providing cheap but nonetheless comfortable accommodation. These days, youth hostels cater for young and old, families, senior citizens and bring people from many different backgrounds together.

In order to use these facilities in Germany, you have to be a member of the German Youth Hostel Association (*Deutsches Jugendherbergswerk*, short: *DJH*) or any other Youth Hostel Association and pay an annual membership fee. The membership card is valid in more than 80 countries around the world and invaluable for those looking for budget accommodation.

Many German youth hostels can be found in stunning locations for example old, mysterious castles and impressive palaces or other historically interesting monuments guaranteeing a unique experience for everyone. In the city of Konstanz, you will find a *Jugendherberge* in a refurbished water tower and in Bremen accommodation for 30 guests is provided in a historic steam ship. In many larger cities, youth hostels take prime position and provide easy, near instant access to important landmarks, something which is generally only available in expensive city centre hotels.

As these examples show each youth hostel is different but they all share a communal value which is to contribute towards intercultural understanding and tolerance.

The Concept of Gemütlichkeit

Some words are notoriously difficult to translate into another language and the German word *Gemütlichkeit* is definitely among them. For lack of a better word, the German term has even been adopted into the English language.

Gemütlichkeit is an abstract noun which describes a feeling of cosiness and a sense of wellbeing in a relaxed environment. However, individual perception plays also a role when trying to define this term. For some, it might imply a well deserved drink with friends after a hard day's work. For others it could simply mean being at home and enjoying some peace and quiet, lying in the bath or attending a local Christmas market. On the list of priorities for German native speakers *Gemütlichkeit* takes a key position and is considered important in a balanced lifestyle.

However, many foreigners associate the term with a slightly different event: the *Oktoberfest* in Munich. Traditional brass music, *Dirndl* and *Lederhosen*, beer and nice food in one of the many beer tents are the first things that come to mind when asked about their idea of *Gemütlichkeit*. The toast *Ein Prosit, ein Prosit der Gemütlichkeit* is without a doubt the most popular song at the *Oktoberfest* and has helped to spread the term *Gemütlichkeit* across the globe.

Apparently, the first English speaker to use the term in the form of the adjective *gemütlich* was Queen Victoria, but then again her mother was German, namely Princess Mary Louise Victoria of Saxe-Coburg-Saalfeld, Princess of Leiningen, Duchess of Kent and Strathearn.

City Breaks in German-Speaking Countries

Graz

In 2003 the city of Graz, Austria's second-largest city after Vienna with a population of around 270,000, took its turn as European Capital of Culture and was transformed into a big stage with many public events taking place. One fascinating project installed for the Cultural Year is the *Murinsel* (the Island in the Mur), a floating shell in the middle of the Mur River connected by two footbridges. The floating island is a link between river and city and creates a unique atmosphere and a stunning backdrop for events or simply a cup of coffee.

Another very unusual building is the *Kunsthaus Graz*, the museum for contemporary art often referred to as the 'friendly alien'. It is best described as a blue balloon or a bubble of air sitting on top of a glass-walled ground floor. It attracts visitors almost as much for the building as for the exhibitions happening within.

Cultural Studies

On a more traditional note, the *Uhrturm* (the clock tower) on the *Schloßberg* (castle hill), the site of an ancient fortress, is the most well known landmark and holds a special place in the hearts of the people of Graz. Built in 1560, the unique design with the distinct wooden roof and the huge clock face are recognisable from afar and give locals and tourists alike their bearings. Huge parts of the *Schloßberg* were destroyed by Napoleons troops, however, the people of Graz refused to see their beloved *Uhrturm* destroyed, so they collectively paid the ransom.

Zürich

The largest city in Switzerland and often voted one of the most desirable cities in the world to live in, Zürich has been continually populated since the Roman times with the first written reference to a Roman customs post in the 9th century. Located on the banks of the Limmat River at the head of Lake Zurich, the city is surrounded by the picturesque, snow-capped Alps.

The *Grossmünster* church (literally: great minster) is one of the three major churches in the city. Construction commenced around 1100, and its inauguration was about 1220. The *Grossmünster* is of special importance as it was the starting point of the Swiss-German Reformation that took place in the first half of the 16th century.

The *Fraumünster* church (literally: woman's minster), founded in 853 by Luis the German, was initially inhabited by aristocratic women from all over Europe. After the reformation, the ownership of the church passed to the city of Zürich. It is well worth a visit as it features beautiful stained glass windows designed by Mark Chagall.

The *Uetliberg* is Zürich's local mountain rising to 869m (2850 feet) above sea level and offering panoramic views of Zürich and surroundings. It is easily accessible by railway from Zürich and it is a paradise for hikers and cyclists in summer and in winter for sledging.

Heidelberg

Looking at pictures of Heidelberg, it becomes immediately apparent why people refer to it as the most romantic city in Germany. The old bridge with the enchanting castle in the background makes a romantic backdrop and inspired many poets, philosophers, singers and songwriter.

Naturally, one of the main attractions is the castle ruin *Schloss Heidelberg* which, without a doubt, is one of the most significant and impressive castles in Germany. The leafy, green hills in the surroundings provide a stunning contrast to the castles' many impressive palaces and towers. Construction started in the 14th century and lasted until the 17th century when it was destroyed by the troops of Louis XIV of France.

The alleyways of the beautiful old town are always full of life, packed with visitors – the city attracts more than three million day-trippers every year – locals and of course students, as Heidelberg is also a well established university city. The *Ruperto Carola Universität*, founded in 1386, is the oldest university in Germany and attracts students from all over the world. It has an excellent reputation and currently hosts over 30,000 students.

Heidelberg, so they say, captures your heart and inspires you to immortalize your own deepest romantic feelings in art. Many will sing the internationally hit song from 1925 *Ich hab' mein Herz in Heidelberg verloren* ('I lost my heart in Heidelberg') when they wave their good-byes to Heidelberg.

Lektion 16: Wir haben hier ein Problem.

1

fest·stecken	*Der Aufzug steckt fest.*	to be stuck
funktionieren	Der Aufzug funktioniert nicht.	to operate, to function, to work
der Gast, ⸚e	Sie sind Gäste im Hotel Maritim.	guest
kennen·lernen	Möchten Sie George Clooney gern kennenlernen?	to get to know
der Kollege, -n	Die beiden sind Kollegen.	colleague
stecken bleiben	*Mit wem möchten Sie im Aufzug stecken bleiben?*	to get stuck

2

die Angst, ⸚e	Die Frau und der Mann haben Angst.	fear
genervt (sein)	*Sie sind genervt.*	(to be) irritated, annoyed
rufen	Sie rufen Hilfe.	to call, to shout
warten	Sie warten.	to wait
weiter·gehen	Wie geht die Geschichte weiter?	to continue, to progress

BILDLEXIKON

der Aufzug, ⸚e	Der Aufzug steckt fest.	lift, elevator
der Bademantel, ⸚	Können Sie mir einen Bademantel bringen?	dressing gown
die Dusche, -n	Die Dusche funktioniert nicht.	shower
der Föhn, -e	*Ich brauche bitte einen Föhn.*	hairdryer
der Fernseher, -	Der Fernseher ist kaputt.	TV
die Heizung, -en	Die Heizung funktioniert nicht.	heating
die Internet-verbindung, -en	Hat das Zimmer eine Internetverbindung?	internet connection
das Licht, -er	Können Sie bitte das Licht ausmachen?	light
die Klimaanlage, -n	Gibt es in dem Hotel keine Klimaanlage?	air conditioning
der Wecker, -	Ich nehme meinen Wecker ins Hotel mit.	alarm clock

> **TIPP** Write little notes and put them all over your flat.

der Wecker   der Fernseher

3

die Aufzugfirma, -firmen	Die Aufzugsfirma kommt in 30 Minuten.	company which produces elevators
aus·machen	Machen Sie bitte das Licht aus.	to turn off
der Hotelgast, ⸚e	Die Hotelgäste warten im Aufzug.	hotel guest
reparieren	Nur die Aufzugsfirma kann den Aufzug reparieren.	to repair
der Techniker, -	*Der Techniker kann helfen.*	technician

Handwritten notes (top):
zuhören: to listen to (pay attention)
hören: listen
Hoffetlich hören Sie mir zu.

tun: (= machen)
tun | Only tun:
tue | Es tut mir leid.
tust |
tut |
tun |
tut |
tun |

Hausaufgaben
Kreuzworträtsel } machen

4

√ kalt	Es ist sehr kalt.	cold
√ kaputt	Der Fernseher ist kaputt.	broken
kümmern: sich √ kümmern um	Ich kümmere mich sofort darum.	to care: to care for
√ schicken	Können Sie einen Techniker schicken?	to send
√ sofort	Ich kümmere mich sofort darum.	straight away

5

√ die Liste, -n	Machen Sie eine Liste mit fünf Dingen.	list
√ mit·nehmen	Ich nehme mein Handy immer mit.	to take sth./so. along

Dusche
Föhn
Klimaanlage

Licht
Wecker
Bett
Fernseher
Heizung
Bademantel
Internet-
verbindung

Handwritten note: Bescheid : decision

6

√ der/die Angestellte, -n	Sie sind Angestellter im Hotel.	employee, staff
Bescheid sagen	Sie sagen dem Zimmermädchen Bescheid.	to let so. know, to give word
√ das Rollenspiel, -e	Rollenspiel: Spielen Sie Gespräche.	role play
√ die Situation, -en	Wählen Sie eine Situation.	situation
√ das Zimmermädchen, -	Das Zimmermädchen bringt sofort Handtücher.	cleaning lady, chamber maid
zweit: zu zweit	*Arbeiten Sie zu zweit.*	*in pairs*

7

√ ab (temporal)	Ab Montag bin ich in Urlaub.	from (one point onward) (temporal)
√ erst	Ich kann erst um 16.30 Uhr kommen.	here: only
√ geehrte/geehrter	Sehr geehrte Frau Wegele, …	dear, honoured (very formal)
√ die Geschäftsreise, -n	Von Mittwoch bis Freitag bin ich auf Geschäfts- reise.	business trip
√ pünktlich	Ich komme leider nicht pünktlich.	punctual, on time
die Sitzung, -en	Ich schaffe es nicht pünktlich zur Sitzung.	meeting

so	Gehen wir essen? So um 18.30 Uhr?	here: (at) about (plus time)
✓ der Tanzkurs, -e	Wir können vor dem Tanzkurs noch zusammen essen.	dance class
✓ das Thema, Themen	Was ist das Thema?	topic
überfliegen	Überfliegen Sie die E-Mails.	to scan, to skim sth. *take a quick look*
✓ der Urlaub, -e	Ich bin für eine Woche im Urlaub.	holiday
✓ der Zeitpunkt, -e	Wann ist ein guter Zeitpunkt?	moment, point in time
die Zukunft (Sg.)	in einer Woche = Zeitpunkt in der Zukunft	future

8

✓ die Alternative, -n	Können Sie eine Alternative vorschlagen?	alternative
✓ der Spanischkurs, -e	Nach dem Spanischkurs habe ich Zeit.	Spanish class
vor·schlagen	Was schlägst du vor?	to suggest
✓ zurück·kommen	Wann kommt Carola zurück?	to return

9

✓ ach, wirklich?	Ich bin im Aufzug stecken geblieben. – Ach, wirklich?	oh really?
✓ dumm	Wie dumm! Jetzt ist das Essen kalt.	silly, stupid
✓ das Navi, -s	Mein Navi funktioniert nicht.	sat nav *GPS, navigator systems*
✓ seltsam	Seltsam! Jetzt funktioniert es doch.	strange

LERNZIELE

✓ für (temporal)	Ich bin für eine Woche im Urlaub.	for (temporal)
✓ nach (temporal)	Petra geht nach der Uni nicht zu Massimo.	after (temporal)
✓ tun	Was kann ich für Sie tun?	to do
vereinbaren	Wollen wir einen Termin für Dienstag vereinbaren?	to agree, to arrange
verschieben	Julia möchte den Termin mit Martin verschieben.	to postpone

Lektion 17: Wer will Popstar werden?

1

die Akademie, -n	Auf der Akademie kann man Singen und Tanzen studieren.	academy
anerkannt	*State* staatlich anerkannte Schule	approved
an·melden (sich)	Melde dich jetzt an!	to register, to subscribe
die Anzeige, -n	Anzeige 1 ist interessant.	advert
die Aufnahmeprüfung, -en	Die Aufnahmeprüfung ist am 15.7.	admission exam, entrance test
bewerben: sich bewerben für	Bewirb dich jetzt für das Casting.	to apply: to apply for
das Casting, -s	Das nächste Casting ist im Juli.	casting
die Castingshow, -s	Die Castingshow sucht den Superstar.	casting show

✓ international	Ich studiere an der internationalen Pop-Akademie.	international
✓ die Schauspiel-kunst, ⸚e	Möchtest du auch auf die Schule für Schauspielkunst?	dramatic arts, academy of drama
✓ staatlich	Ist die Schule staatlich anerkannt?	public, state
✓ der Superstar, -s	Deutschland sucht den Superstar – so heißt eine Castingshow.	super star
✓ werden	Du möchtest Popstar werden.	to become

BILDLEXIKON

✓ das Ausland (Sg.)	Ich habe drei Jahre im Ausland gelebt.	foreign countries (pl.), abroad
✓ (das) Europa	Junge Leute reisen gern durch Europa.	euro
✓ der Führerschein, -e	Stefan möchte bald den Führerschein machen.	driving licence
✓ das Geld (Sg.)	Wer möchte nicht viel Geld haben?	money
✓ heiraten	Martin und Lisa haben geheiratet.	to marry
✓ das Motorrad, ⸚er	Kannst du Motorrad fahren?	motor bike
✓ das (Musik)Instrument, -e	Spielst du ein Musikinstrument?	music instrument
✓ der Politiker, -	Wer will Politiker werden?	politician
✓ reisen	Wir reisen im Sommer durch Europa.	to travel
✓ steigen	Möchtest du auf einen Berg steigen?	to climb
✓ verdienen	Ich möchte viel Geld verdienen.	to earn

ein Buch schreiben

heiraten

im Ausland leben

Chef werden

eine große Familie haben

viele Fremdsprachen lernen

Schauspieler werden

auf einen Berg steigen

den Führerschein machen

Politiker werden

durch Europa reisen

ein Musikinstrument lernen

Geld verdienen

um die Welt segeln

Motorrad fahren

ZUKUNFTSPLÄNE

3

ab·schließen	Hast du die Ausbildung abgeschlossen?	to complete, to finish sth.
besser	Mit einer Berufsausbildung hat man bessere Chancen.	better
die Berufsausbildung, -en	Ich finde eine Berufsausbildung wichtig.	apprenticeship, professional training/education
die Chance, -n	Auch ohne Ausbildung hat Cherry sehr gute Chancen.	chance
dort	Lisa war auf zwei Musikschulen, aber dort hat sie nicht viel gelernt.	there
einfach (Modalpartikel)	Mit der Pop-Akademie habe ich einfach bessere Chancen.	here: simply (modal particle)
das Glück (Sg.): Glück bringen	Die Starbrille bringt Cherry Glück.	luck: to bring luck
das Image, -s	*Was kann ich für mein Image tun?*	*image*
jung	289 junge Leute haben sich angemeldet.	young
das Komponieren	*Auf der Akademie kann man Komponieren lernen.*	*composing*
der Liedermacher, -	Fabian sagt, er ist Liedermacher.	song writer
die Musikproduktion, -en	Was ist wichtig für die Musikproduktion?	music production
die Musikschule, -n	Lisa war auf zwei Musikschulen.	music school, conservatoire
PR (Public Relations)	*PR – Wie arbeitet man richtig mit Internet, Radio, Fernsehen und Zeitungen?*	*PR (public relations)*
der Profi, -s	Ich will schnell Profi werden.	professional (short: pro)
der Singer-Songwriter, -	*Die meisten Leute sagen „Singer-Songwriter" und nicht „Liedermacher".*	*singer-songwriter*
die Starbrille, -n	Sehen Sie mal: Das ist meine Starbrille.	glasses fit for a star
der Studienplatz, ̈e	Nur 12 bekommen einen Studienplatz an der Pop-Akademie.	university place
der Textanfang, ̈e	Lesen Sie den Textanfang.	beginning of a text
texten	*Fabian textet und singt nur auf Deutsch.*	*to write a songtext*
verkaufen: sich verkaufen	Wie verkaufe ich mich?	to sell: to sell yourself
weiter·lesen	Lesen Sie nun den Text weiter.	to read on
zählen	Für sie zählt heute nur eine Frage.	to count

TIPP Find words for a specific topic.

Musik: Sänger, Lied, Instrument spielen, singen, tanzen, Konzert

4

jeweils	Notieren Sie jeweils drei Gegenstände.	each, in each case
die Kreditkarte, -n	Ich nehme meine Kreditkarte mit.	credit card
das Lieblingsbuch, ¨er	Wie heißt dein Lieblingsbuch?	favourite book
die Prüfung, -en	Hast du Angst vor der Prüfung?	exam
das Prüfungszimmer, -	Fabian geht in das Prüfungszimmer.	exam room

6

der Fall, ¨e: auf keinen Fall	Ich will auf keinen Fall Motorrad fahren.	case: in no case, no chance

7

der Abschluss, ¨e	Schreiben Sie zwei Wörter zum Abschluss.	conclusion
die Anleitung, -en	Lesen Sie die Anleitung.	instruction
das Elfchen-Gedicht, -e	„Elfchen"-Gedichte sind Gedichte mit elf Wörtern.	short poem consisting of eleven words
fit (sein)	Bist du fit?	(to be) fit
das Gedicht, -e	Ich möchte gern Gedichte schreiben.	poem
gemütlich	Mit den Nachbarn ist es so gemütlich.	comfortable
der iPod, -s®	Hast du einen iPod?	ipod®
laufen	Ich laufe am Mittwoch im Park.	to run
putzen	Die Wohnung putzen – wie langweilig!	to clean
die Zeile, -n	Das Gedicht hat fünf Zeilen.	line

LERNZIELE

äußern	Sie äußern ihre Wünsche.	to express
kreativ	kreatives Schreiben	creative
unbedingt	Ich will unbedingt Schauspielerin werden.	absolutely, at all costs
der Wunsch, ¨e	Wir sprechen im Kurs über Wünsche.	wish
der Zeitungstext, -e	Lesen Sie den Zeitungstext.	newspaper article

Lektion 18: Geben Sie ihm doch diesen Tee!

1

die Kopfschmerzen (Pl.)	Herr Brehm hat Kopfschmerzen.	headache
krank sein	Er ist krank.	to be ill

BILDLEXIKON

die Apotheke, -n	In der Apotheke bekommen Sie Medikamente.	pharmacy
das Fieber (Sg.)	Das Fieber ist nicht sehr hoch.	fever, temperature
der Husten (Sg.)	Was tun Sie bei Husten?	cough

✓ das Medikament, -e	Ich brauche ein Medikament gegen Kopf-schmerzen.	medicine, drug
✓ das Pflaster, -	Hast du ein Pflaster?	plaster 石膏
✓ die Praxis, Praxen	Der Arzt arbeitet in einer Praxis.	surgery
✓ das Rezept, -e	Für das Medikament brauchen Sie ein Rezept.	prescription
die Salbe, -n	Mein Rücken tut weh. Haben Sie vielleicht eine Salbe?	ointment 软膏
der Schnupfen, -	Ich habe Schnupfen.	cold
✓ die Tablette, -n	Ich nehme eine Tablette oder gehe zum Arzt.	pill

2

✓ der Arm, -e	Hat er auch Schmerzen in den Armen?	arm
✓ das Bein, -e	Mein Bein tut weh.	leg
✓ bleiben	Ich bleibe im Bett.	to remain, to stay
✓ hoch	Das Fieber ist hoch.	high
husten	Er hustet und hustet. Er hat Husten.	to cough

3

der Beitrag, ⸚e	Lesen Sie die Beiträge im Gesundheitsforum.	here: article
✓ das Vitamin C	Nehmen Sie Vitamin C.	vitamin C

4

der Bauch, ⸚e	Mein Bauch tut weh.	stomach
die Brust, ⸚e	Sie hat Schmerzen in der Brust.	chest
der Finger, -	Die Hand hat fünf Finger.	finger
der Fuß, ⸚e	Ein Mensch hat zwei Füße.	foot
der Hals, ⸚e	*sage* Salbei ist gut für den Hals.	throat
die Hand, ⸚e	Ich habe immer noch Schmerzen in der Hand.	hand
das Knie, -	Au, mein Knie!	knee
der Mund, ⸚er	Sein Mund ist groß.	mouth
die Nase, -n	Ihre Nase ist klein.	nose
das Ohr, -en	Er hat große Ohren.	ear
der Zahn, ⸚e	Sie hat Zahnschmerzen.	tooth

> **TIPP**
> Now play a memo game with words about *health and illness*. Write a sentence on two cards, mix them and find the pairs.

Mein Bein | tut weh.

Ich habe | Husten und Schnupfen.

Ich bin | krank.

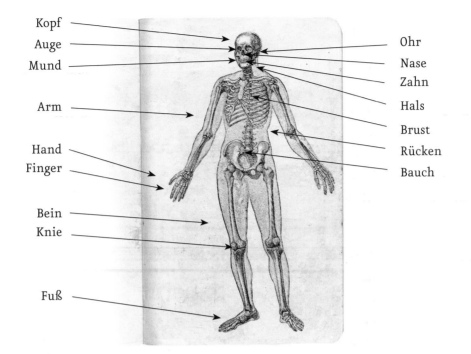

Kopf — Ohr
Auge — Nase
Mund — Zahn
Arm — Hals
Hand — Brust
Finger — Rücken
Bein — Bauch
Knie
Fuß

5

der Baldrian, -e	Baldrian ist gut bei Kopf- oder Bauchschmerzen.	valerian 颂草
bei	Was machen Sie bei Kopfschmerzen?	here: for
erscheinen	Das Buch ist im Kloster-Verlag erschienen.	here: to be published
fein	Gutes und Feines aus dem Kloster	fine 精
die Halsschmerzen (Pl.)	Salbei hilft sehr gut gegen Halsschmerzen.	sore throat
das Heilkraut, ¨er	Nehmen Sie doch mal Heilkräuter.	medicinal herb
der Kamillentee, -s	Gegen Bauchschmerzen trinke ich Kamillentee.	camomille tea 洋甘菊
das Kloster, ¨	Schwester Angelika lebt in einem Kloster.	monastery, cloister 修道院
der Klosterladen, ¨	Der Klosterladen Bieberach verkauft Heilkräuter.	monastery shop
der Klosterlikör, -e	Der Klosterlikör schmeckt sehr gut.	herbal liqueur brewed by a monastery
die Kosmetika (Pl.)	Im Klosterladen gibt es auch Kosmetika.	cometics
der Kräutertee, -s	Ich trinke Kräutertee gegen Fieber.	herbal tea
die Küchenkräuter (Pl.)	Mit Küchenkräutern kochen – das macht das Essen besser.	culinary herbs
die Naturmedizin (Sg.)	Oft kann Ihnen auch die Naturmedizin helfen.	natural medicine
der Ratgebertext, -e	Lesen Sie den Ratgebertext.	text giving advice
der Salbei (Sg.)	Oft helfen auch Heilkräuter, zum Beispiel Salbei.	sage
die Spirituosen (Pl.)	Im Klosterladen gibt es auch Spirituosen.	spirits, alcohols
der Verlag, -e	Das Buch ist im Kloster-Verlag erschienen.	publisher

6

befragen	Befragen Sie Ihren Partner.	to interview
dritt: zu dritt	Arbeiten Sie zu dritt.	in sets of three
gesund	Wie gesund lebst du?	healthy
die Umfrage, -n	Machen Sie eine Umfrage im Kurs.	survey

zu zweite. (handwritten note)

7

die Fantasiefigur, -en	Zeichnen Sie eine Fantasiefigur.	fantasy figure
die Figur (Sg.)	Beschreiben Sie Ihre Figur.	figure
das Haar, -e	Ihre Haare sind lang.	hair
das Spiel, -e	Spielen Sie das Spiel.	game
die Zeichnung, -en	Welche Zeichnungen passen zusammen?	drawing

fit (handwritten note)

LERNZIELE

die Bauchschmerzen (Pl.)	Was machst du gegen Bauchschmerzen?	stomachache
gegen	Gegen Bauchschmerzen trinke ich Tee.	here: for, against
der Imperativ, -e	Imperativ: Gehen Sie zum Arzt!	imperative
der Kopf, ⁻e	Mein Kopf tut weh.	head
das Körperteil, -e	Körperteile: Arm, Bein, Kopf …	body part
die Krankheit, -en	Ich spreche nicht gern über Krankheiten. Du?	illness
der Ratgeber, -	Lesen Sie den Ratgeber(text)!	advice booklet, guidebook
der Ratschlag, ⁻e	Welche Ratschläge gibt Schwester Angelika?	advice
der Schmerz, -en	Haben Sie Schmerzen?	pain
sollen	Schwester Angelika sagt, du sollst im Bett bleiben.	should, supposed to
weh·tun	Mein Kopf tut weh.	to ache, to hurt

GRAMMATIK & KOMMUNIKATION

direkt	direkt: Geben Sie ihm diesen Tee!	direct
indirekt	indirekt: Schwester Angelika sagt, ich soll dir diesen Tee geben.	indirect
der Sport (Sg.)	Dann soll er Sport machen.	sport
die Verwendung, -en	Verwendung von Imperativ und sollen	usage, application

MODUL-PLUS LESEMAGAZIN

1

der Anwalt, ⁻e	Ich gebe die Sache an meinen Anwalt.	lawyer
der Apparat, -e	Um 16.05 Uhr war ein Mann am Apparat.	here: phone; also: device, machine
berechnen	Für diesen Service berechnen wir 25 Euro.	to charge
das Betriebssystem, -e	MigaFlex Ultra 1.02 läuft auf allen Betriebssystemen.	operating system

√ die Dame, -n	Sehr geehrte Damen und Herren, ...	lady
√ deinstallieren	Ich möchte das Programm deinstallieren.	to deinstall, to uninstall
deshalb	Deshalb möchte ich mein Geld zurück.	therefore, hence
√ der Erfolg, -e	Ich habe noch einmal angerufen, ohne Erfolg.	success
das Festnetz, -e	0,49 Euro / Minute aus dem Festnetz	landline
√ toll	Ich finde meine Uhr toll.	great
√ installieren	Einfach installieren und problemlos nutzen!	to install
√ die Internet-Seite, -n	Auf Ihrer Internet-Seite versprechen Sie: alles ganz einfach!	internet page
√ der Kaufpreis, -e	Der Kaufpreis ist 199 Euro.	purchase price
√ langsam	Mein Computer läuft ganz langsam.	slow
löschen	Ich will die Software löschen.	to delete
√ der Mitarbeiter, - die Mitarbeiterin, -nen	Ihr Mitarbeiter hat keine Zeit.	co-worker, colleague
√ das Monatsende, -n	Überweisen Sie mir das Geld bis zum Monatsende.	end of month, ultimo
√ nutzen	Die Software können Sie sofort nutzen.	to utilise
√ das Online-Handbuch, ¨er	Das Online-Handbuch versteht kein Mensch.	online handbook
√ problemlos	Man kann die Software nicht problemlos installieren.	easily, trouble-free
der Sachbearbeiter, -	Die Sachbearbeiter sind in der Mittagspause.	official in charge (e.g. adviser, consultant, clerk, case worker)
√ der Service, -s	Die Firma hat einen schlechten Service.	service
√ die Service-Abteilung, -en	Die Service-Abteilung ist geschlossen.	service department
√ die Software (Sg.)	Vor einer Woche habe ich Ihre Software gekauft.	software
√ die Telefon-Hotline, -s	Bei Fragen hilft unsere Telefon-Hotline.	helpline
√ die Telefonkosten (Pl.)	Ich möchte die Telefonkosten zurück.	telephone costs/expenses (pl.)
√ verlieren	Ich will auf keinen Fall noch mehr Geld verlieren.	to lose
√ versprechen	Auf Ihrer Internet-Seite versprechen Sie viel.	to promise
√ versuchen	Ich habe Sie dreimal angerufen. Um 16.05 Uhr habe ich es noch einmal versucht.	to try
weiter·geben	Ich gebe die Sache meinem Anwalt weiter.	to pass on
√ die Wirklichkeit, -en	So sieht die Wirklichkeit aus.	reality
zurück·überweisen	Bitte überweisen Sie das Geld zurück.	to transfer back

überweisen: transfer (auf, an + acc to) -

MODUL-PLUS FILM-STATIONEN

1

√ der Busch, ¨e	Er schneidet Büsche.	bush
√ der Elektroinstallateur, -e	Nach der Schule hat er Elektroinstallateur gelernt.	electrician
√ die Elektronikfirma, -firmen	Er arbeitet bei einer Elektronikfirma.	electronics company

der Hausmeister, -	Heute arbeitet er als Hausmeister.	janitor
die Hecke, -n	Er schneidet die Hecken.	hedge
der Strom (Sg.)	Er kümmert sich um das Wasser und den Strom.	electricity
die Tür, -en	Er repariert Türen.	door

2

die Karriere, -n	Ich will Karriere machen.	career
die Krücke, -n	Ich will endlich wieder ohne Krücken gehen.	crutch
das Model, -s	Junge Frauen möchten oft Model werden.	model
der Tierarzt, ⸚e	Mein Sohn will Tierarzt werden.	veterinarian

3

das Joggen	Ich gehe zwei oder drei Mal pro Woche joggen.	to go fo a run
die Meditation, -en	Joggen ist für mich Meditation.	meditation
morgens	Ich sitze von morgens bis abends am Computer.	in the morning
pro: einmal pro Woche	Wie oft joggst du pro Woche?	per: once a week

MODUL-PLUS PROJEKT LANDESKUNDE

1

begleiten	Wünsche begleiten unser Leben.	to accompany
die Erde (Sg.)	Der Baum symbolisiert die Verbindung zwischen Himmel und Erde.	earth
die Gesundheit (Sg.)	Mein großer Wunsch? Gesundheit.	health
die Liebe (Sg.)	Viele Menschen haben einen Wunsch: Liebe.	love
der Millionär, -e	Ich will Millionär werden.	millionaire
symbolisieren	Was symbolisiert der Wunschbaum?	to symbolize
die Verbindung, -en	Der Baum symbolisiert die Verbindung zwischen Himmel und Erde.	connection
die Weltreise, -n	Ich möchte so gern eine Weltreise machen.	round-the-world trip
der Wunschbaum, ⸚e	In vielen Ländern gibt es den Wunschbaum.	wishing tree
wünschen (sich)	Ich wünsche mir ein Haus am Meer.	to wish
zahlreich	Jeder hat zahlreiche Wünsche.	numerous

2

erfolgreich	Ich will beruflich erfolgreich sein.	successful
die Hauptsache (Sg.)	Hauptsache, die Arbeit macht Spaß.	main issue
reich	Ich will unbedingt reich werden.	rich
das Segelboot, -e	Ich will ein Segelboot haben.	sail boat, sailing boat
der Sportwagen, -	Ich will auch einen Sportwagen haben.	sports car

4

✓ das Lotto, -s	*Spiel doch Lotto!*	lottery

MODUL-PLUS AUSKLANG

1

✓ der Chor, ⁈e	*Der Chor singt: Gloria, Viktoria …*	choir
✓ der Chor-Text, -e	*Lesen Sie den Chor-Text.*	choir lyrics
✓ der Dienst, -e	Doktor Eisenbarth hat seine Dienste angeboten.	service
halt *(Modalpartikel)*	*Schlafen Sie halt am Tag.*	modal particle, does not translate literally, may express resignation (used mainly in spoken language)
✓ der Hauptplatz, ⁈e	Als mobiler Arzt hat er auf dem Hauptplatz seine Dienste angeboten.	main square
✓ der Helfer, -	*Er ist mit seinen Helfern von Ort zu Ort gefahren.*	helper, assistant
das Huhn, ⁈er	Hühner legen Eier.	chicken
✓ mobil	Doktor Eisenbarth war ein mobiler Arzt.	mobil
✓ na gut	*Meine Arbeit stresst mich. – Na gut, dann arbeiten Sie nicht mehr.*	okay then, fair enough
✓ die Originalmelodie, -n	*Wir haben die Originalmelodie genommen, aber den Text neu geschrieben.*	original melody
✓ der Patient, -en	Die Therapien sind schlecht für die Patienten.	patient
✓ per: per Telefon	*Er gibt seine Ratschläge per Telefon.*	by phone
✓ der Rat (Sg.)	Ich brauche Ihren Rat.	advice
recht *(Modalpartikel)*	Er hat seine Arbeit recht gut gemacht.	fairly (modal particle, conveys the speaker's attitude towards the message)
✓ sogar	Ein paar Patienten sterben sogar.	even
✓ sterben	Im Lied ist er kein guter Arzt: Seine Patienten sterben.	to die
✓ stressen	*Meine Arbeit stresst mich sehr.*	to stress
✓ die Therapie, Therapien	*Hilft diese Therapie?*	therapy
✓ der Tod, -e	Nach seinem Tod haben Studenten ein Lied geschrieben.	death

2

dichten	Dichten Sie neue ~~Strophen~~ *Verse.* *die*	to write poetry

Grammar Explanations

Lektion 16: Wir haben hier ein Problem.

Temporal prepositions vor, nach, in *and* für

Vor (*before, ago*) refers to a moment before another point in time or event.

Ich habe mein Handy **vor einem Jahr** gekauft.	*I bought my mobile a year* **ago.**
Vor dem Tanzkurs können wir etwas essen.	*We can eat* **before** *the dance class.*

Nach (*after*) refers to a moment after another point in time or event.

Nach einem Jahr in Italien spricht sie sehr gut Italienisch.	**After** *a year in Italy she speaks Italian very well.*
Nach den Sitzungen gehe ich nach Hause.	**After** *the meetings I am going home.*

In (*in*) always refers to a moment in the future.

Der Kurs beginnt **in einer Woche**.	*The course starts* **in** *a week.*

Für (*for*) refers to a time span / period of time from now on or in the future. Very often it indicates time spent away, on a trip or holidays.

Wir fahren **für einen Monat** in die Schweiz.	*We are going to Switzerland* **for** *a month.*

Vor and **in**, used as temporal prepositions, both require the **dative case.**

Nach *always requires the* **dative case.**
Für *always requires the* **accusative case.**

Lektion 17: Wer will Popstar werden?

Prepositions mit *and* ohne

Preposition **mit** is used like the English *with* and always requires the **dative case.**

Cherry geht **mit ihrer Starbrille** in die Prüfung.	*Cherry goes to the exam* **with** *her star glasses on.*

Preposition **ohne** is used like the English *without* and always requires the accusative case.

Fabian geht **ohne seine Gitarre** in die Prüfung.	*Fabian goes to the exam* **without** *his guitar.*

Modal auxiliary wollen

The verb **wollen** is one of the modal auxiliaries (Modalverben) and is used to express the things that we definitely **want** to do or to have.

		wollen			
singular	ich	**will**	plural	wir	wollen
	du	**willst**		ihr	wollt
	er/sie	**will**		sie/Sie	wollen

Like other modal auxiliaries in German the verb **wollen** is often used with the **infinitive** of another verb. The infinitive is placed at the end of the sentence and builds **the sentence bracket**.

Wer **will** Popstar **werden**?   *Who **wants to become** a pop star?*
Fabian **will** Musik **studieren**.   *Fabian **wants to study** music.*

Sentence bracket

In a known or obvious context, **wollen** can be also used without another verb in infinitive:

Ich **will** einen Laptop.   *I **want** a laptop. (I want to have it, to get it, to buy it etc...)*

The verb werden

The verb **werden** (*to become*) is irregular and has a vowel change **e → i**. It is often used in the infinitive form together with a modal auxiliary.

		werden			
singular	ich	werde	plural	wir	werden
	du	wirst		ihr	werdet
	er/sie	wird		sie/Sie	werden

Was möchtest du **werden**?   *What would you like to become?*
Ich will Sängerin **werden**!   *I want to become a singer!*

Lektion 18: Geben Sie ihm doch diesen Tee!

The imperative

The imperative mood is used to express **a command or a plea**, sometimes a **suggestion**. The speaker is addressing someone directly. The easiest form is the official / formal one – the imperative form for the **Sie-person**.

Geben Sie ihm diesen Tee!   *Give him this tee!*
Trinken Sie viel!   *Drink a lot!*

The word order in these sentences is the same as in yes- / no-questions.

Grammar Explanations

Modal auxiliary sollen

The verb **sollen** is one of the modal auxiliaries and it is used to express the things that we should do / we are obligated to do.

		sollen			
singular	ich	**soll**	plural	wir	sollen
	du	**sollst**		ihr	sollt
	er/sie	**soll**		sie/Sie	sollen

Like other modal auxiliaries in German, the verb **sollen** is used with the **infinitive** of another verb. The infinitive is placed at the end of the sentence and builds the **sentence bracket**.

Du **sollst** zum Arzt **gehen**.   You **should go** to the doctor.

Sentence bracket

The verb **sollen** can be used as an alternative for the imperative mood. By using **sollen**, the suggestion or command is expressed in a more indirect way.

Geben Sie ihm diesen Tee. → Sie **sollen** ihm diesen Tee **geben**!   *You should give him this tea!*
Trinken Sie viel!   → Sie **sollen** viel **trinken**!   *You should drink a lot!*

The preposition gegen

The preposition **gegen** (*against / for*) is often used in the health / medical context.

Was hilft **gegen Bauchschmerzen**?   *What helps against / for stomach pain?*
Gegen Kopfschmerzen nehme ich   *I always take a tablet against / for headache.*
  immer eine Tablette.

Word forming with -schmerzen

The plural form of the noun *pain* → Schmerzen added to a body part or parts is used to describe suffering from pain in this body part.

Ich habe **Kopfschmerzen**.   *I have a headache.*
Ich habe **Zahnschmerzen**.   *I have a toothache.*
Ich habe **Halsschmerzen**.   *I have a sore throat.*

The phrase Sport machen

In the phrase *to play sports*, the German noun **Sport** is used in **singular**, together with the verb **machen**, <u>not</u> spielen:

Man soll viel **Sport machen**.   *One should play sports a lot.*

Asking for Help in German

Being polite is always important, especially when asking for help. English speakers normally use different phrases to soften their request unlike German speakers who usually prefer to come to the point straight away.

Germans are a lot more direct than English speakers would be and there is often a communication clash between British indirectness and German directness. In German, one can simply say *Bring mir bitte das Buch*, whereas English speakers are highly likely to soften the request by first saying 'Could you do me a favour...?' or 'Would you mind ...?'. German efficiency in communication is focused on communicating a point promptly without adding unnecessary softening words or polite small talk beforehand.

So always remember: neither German speakers nor English speakers mean to be rude, it all simply comes down to different rules of communication.

Sebastian Kneipp — the Nature's Advocate

"Nature has provided us generously with everything we need to remain in good health." – Sebastian Kneipp

Sebastian Kneipp (1821–1897), a Bavarian priest and naturopath, had a great influence on the world of medicine with his holistic healing approach and was one of the founders of a natural cure movement.

Born in 1821, he trained as a weaver initially in order to follow his father's profession, but when he was 23, he decided to become a priest. Soon afterwards, Sebastian Kneipp fell ill with a severe case of tuberculosis which at that time was considered a deadly disease. Kneipp, after having found a book on hydrotherapy, started self-treatment and immersed himself into the freezing cold waters of the Danube several times a week in order to strengthen his immune system and cured himself. He claimed to have used the healing powers of plants and water and created his own life philosophy. Once he was cured, Sebastian Kneipp performed a series of tests on himself and his patients with the purpose to refine his treatment and he was very successful in curing people from their illnesses. However, word soon spread and some pharmacists and doctors accused him of charlatanism but the successful tests proved him right. From 1855 onwards, Sebastian Kneipp lived in Bad Wörishofen, a small town in Bavaria which due to Kneipp's popularity attracted more and more spa tourists and people looking for help with their ill health.

Kneipp's philosophy is based on five elements: water, plants, diet, exercise and inner balance. His water treatment proved especially successful and it still used up to this day as a very popular natural healing method. The application of hot and cold water, working with water pressure and water stepping are all examples of hydrotherapeutic methods that are still in use.

Health Care in Austria, Germany and Switzerland

Looking at the healthcare system in Austria, Switzerland and Germany, it is apparent that they have one trait in common: a very high standard of care, both public and private, generally exceeding international health care standards.

The Austrian health care system is often perceived to be one of the best publicly funded national health care programs. It offers users high-quality health care with the opportunity to pay for supplementary private insurance for added comforts such as a private room in hospital and for more flexibility with visiting hours. Private health care is also available if one wishes.

The level of employment determines how much one has to pay with higher earners paying higher contributions and in all cases the firm contributes half and the employee the other half. Children and other dependants are automatically covered through the insurance of the employed family member.

The Austrian law is generally very strict about the prescription of drugs; many over-the-counter drugs in other countries are only available by prescription. A prescription, in German known as a *Rezept*, will be given by a consultant or doctor and in most cases patients only have to pay a small fee, called *Zuzahlungspflicht* (additional contribution), which is currently 5.30 euro and the *Gebietskrankenkasse* (public health insurance) pays for the remaining cost of drugs. Private patients must pay the full amount but they can claim a refund for the cost from their insurance.

Historically, the German health care system is the first universal health care system and after World War II many other European countries followed the German model.

More than 80% of Germans have a *gesetzliche Krankenversicherung* which means they are covered under the national health system as opposed to the *private Krankenversicherung*. Dental treatment can be very expensive and as it is not always covered in the standard medical insurance, many Germans take out an additional private insurance.

Patients who are enrolled in the public health system do not have to pay the full cost for prescriptions; they pay 10% of the total cost. Medication can only be picked up in pharmacies, in German known as *Apotheken*, and it is interesting to note that Germany is the biggest pharmacy market in Europe. Many foreigners notice that there is a huge abundance of pharmacies in German cities. In some places, there literally seems to be one on every corner.

The Swiss health care system is slightly different as is not tax based and not partly financed by the employer. Health care has to be organised on an individual basis and each person is free to choose their own insurer. Insurance companies are not allowed to refuse an applicant regardless of age and previous health history. Within three months of arrival into the country, individuals are obliged to have a health insurance provider with the only exemption being those that are staying less than three months.

People with basic health insurance contribute 10% of the cost of medication and otherwise the mandatory basic system covers a wide variety of treatments. Similar to Germany and Austria, many people take out supplementary health insurance for additional treatments such as dental care.

Many consider the Swiss health system to be the best in the world as there are short waiting lists, well-equipped hospitals and access to plenty of doctors and specialists. For many reasons it is often taken as a role model for other countries.

Lektion 19: Der hatte doch keinen Bauch!

BILDLEXIKON

✓blond	Kerstin ist blond.	blond
✓dick	Walter hat einen Bauch, er ist ein bisschen dick.	big, fat
✓dünn	Models sind oft viel zu dünn.	thin, skinny
✓glatt	Ich habe glatte Haare, aber ich möchte lieber Locken.	here: straight
✓grau	Meine Großeltern haben graue Haare.	grey
✓hübsch	Deine Augen, deine Haare – du bist wirklich sehr hübsch!	beautiful, pretty
✓ *die Locke, -n*	*Hanna hat braune Locken.*	*curl*
✓schlank	Ich bin nicht dick! Ich bin schlank.	slim

Bart — blonde Haare — dünn/schlank

lange Haare — braune Haare — dick

kurze Haare — schwarze Haare — hübsch

glatte Haare — graue Haare — hässlich

Locken

AUSSEHEN

4

✓freundlich	Helga ist sehr freundlich.	friendly
✓fröhlich	Nina lacht immer. Sie ist sehr fröhlich.	cheerful
✓komisch	Ich finde, Udo ist komisch.	strange
✓sympathisch	Angela ist sympathisch. Alle mögen sie.	likeable
✓traurig	Du siehst heute so traurig aus. Was ist los?	sad
✓unfreundlich	Unser Hausmeister ist immer so unfreundlich.	unfriendly
✓unglücklich	Die Frau sieht sehr unglücklich aus.	unhappy

√ uninteressant	Das Buch ist total uninteressant.	dull
√ unsympathisch	Mike ist unsympathisch. Er denkt nur an sich.	dislikable, unfriendly

TIPP Use visuable images and create word-pictures.

vergessen   *schlank*

5

√ der Bürokaufmann, Bürokaufleute	*Klaus war früher Bürokaufmann.*	office administrator
√ ledig	Simone ist ledig.	single
√ der Musiker, -	Heute ist Klaus Musiker.	musician
√ die Sekretärin, -nen	Sie hat früher als Sekretärin gearbeitet.	secretary (female)
√ die Yoga-Lehrerin, -nen	*Heute arbeitet sie als Yoga-Lehrerin.*	yoga teacher (female)

6

√ beschweren (sich)	*Die Nachbarn haben sich beschwert.* Es war zu laut.	to complain
√ die Diskothek, -en	Ich habe früher in einer Diskothek gearbeitet.	disco, night club
√ erkennen	Erkennst du mich nicht? Ich bin es: Tim!	to recognize
√ laut	Die Musik ist zu laut. Ich kann nicht schlafen.	loud, noisy

7

√ die Bäckerei, -en	Mein Vater hatte eine Bäckerei.	bakery
√ die Hausfrau, -en	Meine Mutter war Hausfrau.	housewife
√ die (Lügen-) Geschichte, -n	Erzählen Sie eine (Lügen-) Geschichte.	made-up story
√ die Sache, -n	Er hat eine Geschichte erzählt, aber eine Sache war falsch.	thing

8

√ ach komm!	*Das war vor 8 Jahren. – Ach komm, da hatten wir schon keinen Kontakt mehr.*	come on!
√ ach was!	*Das ist Walter! – Ach was! Der hatte doch keinen Bart.*	nonsense!
√ ach du liebe Zeit!	*Ach du liebe Zeit! Er ist es wirklich.*	oh dear!
√ die Luxus-Disco, -s	*Mike hat diese Luxus-Disco in Grünwald gehört.*	luxury disco
√ tausendmal	*Er hat sich tausendmal entschuldigt.*	a thousand times
√ Wahnsinn!	*Sylvie will nicht mehr mit ihm zusammen sein. – Wahnsinn!*	Man!

LERNZIELE

√ das Aussehen (Sg.)	*Beschreiben Sie das Aussehen.*	appearance, looks (pl.)
√ der Bart, ⸚e	Er hatte doch keinen Bart!	beard

✓ der Charakter, Charaktere	Beschreiben Sie eine Person. Wie ist ihr Charakter?	character
✓ echt?	Es gibt die Disco nicht mehr. – Echt?	really?
✓ erstaunt	A erzählt eine Geschichte. B und C reagieren erstaunt.	amazed, astonished
✓ das Präteritum, Präterita	Präteritum: war, hatte	simple past
✓ der Smalltalk, -s	Auf einer Party machen die Leute Smalltalk.	small talk

Lektion 20: Komm sofort runter!

2

✓ der Brief, -e	Line schreibt einen Brief.	letter
✓ runter·kommen	Line soll runterkommen.	to come down

3

✓ das Tagebuch, ⸚er	Schreiben Sie Tagebuch?	diary

BILDLEXIKON

✓ der Abfall, ⸚e	Wer bringt den Abfall raus?	waste, rubbish, garbage
✓ ab·trocknen	Trocknest du bitte ab?	to dry, to towel down
✓ abwaschen	Wer wäscht heute ab?	to wash the dishes
✓ auf·hängen	Häng bitte die Wäsche auf.	to hang up (washing)
✓ aus·räumen	Räum die Spülmaschine aus. – Immer ich!	to empty, to clear out sth.
✓ der Boden, ⸚	Jeden Abend wischt Ella den Boden in der Küche.	floor
✓ bügeln	Bei uns bügelt mein Mann.	to iron
✓ das Geschirr (Sg.)	Ich wasche das Geschirr nicht selbst ab, ich habe eine Spülmaschine.	dishes (pl.)
✓ raus·bringen	Bitte bring den Müll raus.	to take outside
✓ spülen	Geschirr spülen, nein danke! – Dann kauf doch eine Spülmaschine.	to wash
✓ die Spülmaschine, -n	Ist die Spülmaschine schon fertig? Dann räum sie bitte aus.	dishwasher
✓ staubsaugen	Staubsaugen – das mache ich immer am Samstag.	to vacuum-clean
✓ die Wäsche (Sg.)	Ich habe heute Wäsche gewaschen.	laundry, washing
✓ waschen	Vor dem Essen Hände waschen!	to wash
✓ wischen	Der Boden ist sehr schmutzig. Wisch ihn bitte.	to wash the floor

Fenster putzen

Geschirr abwaschen/abtrocknen

den Müll/Abfall rausbringen

Wäsche waschen

den Boden wischen

TIPP Find words with the same or a similar meaning.

spülen — abwaschen

4

✓ faul	Seid nicht so faul!	lazy
✓ die Hausaufgabe, -n	Vergiss deine Hausaufgaben nicht!	homework
✓ die Mama, -s	*Keine andere Mutter ist so, nur Mama.*	*mum, mama*
✓ Mist!	*Ich soll das Bad putzen. Mist!*	*Bugger!*
✓ na los!	*Na los! Steht endlich auf.*	come on! ✓
✓ nerven	*Mama nervt.*	to annoy so.
Oh nein!	*Oh nein! Was will sie den jetzt schon wieder?*	oh no!
✓ peinlich	Das war so peinlich!	embarassing

6

das Bewegungsspiel, -e	Wir spielen ein Bewegungsspiel im Kurs.	activity game
✓ formulieren	*Formulieren Sie Bitten.*	*to write sth. up*

7

✓ der Anrufbeantworter, -	Auf dem Anrufbeantworter ist ein Anruf von Peter.	answering machine
✓ auf (sein)	Meine Fenster sind alle auf.	to (be) open
✓ ihn	Ruf ihn bitte zurück.	him (accusative, 3rd pers. sing.)
✓ mich	*Kannst du mich abholen?*	*me (personal pronoun, accusative)*
✓ sauber	Ich habe das Bad geputzt. Jetzt ist es sauber.	clean
✓ schmutzig	Das Bad war sehr schmutzig.	dirty
✓ die Wohngemeinschaft, -en	Studenten leben oft in einer Wohngemeinschaft.	flat share

auf machen

✓ zu·machen	Mach bitte die Fenster zu.	to close
✓ zurück·rufen	Du sollst Peter zurückrufen.	to call back

8

✓ *gegenseitig*	*Korrigieren Sie gegenseitig Ihre Sätze.*	*each other*

9

✓ der Dreck (Sg.)	Ich hasse Unordnung und Dreck.	dirt
✓ freiwillig	Du putzt freiwillig Bad und Küche.	voluntary
✓ *gründlich*	*Ich putze gern und gründlich.*	*thoroughly*
✓ hassen	Ich hasse Bügeln.	to hate
✓ *der Mitbewohner, -*	*Franzi sucht einen Mitbewohner für ihre WG.*	*flatmate, cohabitant*
✓ ordentlich	Ich bin ordentlich und räume jeden Tag auf.	tidy
✓ supergünstig	Die Wohnung ist supergünstig.	very cheap
✓ die Terrasse, -n	Die Wohnung ist im Erdgeschoss und hat eine Terrasse.	terrace
✓ die Traumwohnung, -en	Meine Traumwohnung hat einen Balkon.	dream flat
✓ die Unordnung (Sg.)	Ich finde Unordnung nicht so schlimm.	mess, disorder
✓ wahnsinnig	Ich koche wahnsinnig gern.	here: incredibly
✓ *das WG-Zimmer, -*	*Das WG-Zimmer ist sehr günstig.*	*room in a shared flat*
✓ die Zimmergröße, -n	Zimmergröße: 20 m²	room size

LERNZIELE

die Aufforderung, -en	Bitten und Aufforderungen: Deck bitte den Tisch.	request, invitation
✓ *decken*	*Deck bitte den Tisch.*	*here: to set the table*
✓ der Haushalt, (-e)	Line soll ihrer Mutter im Haushalt helfen.	household
der Tagebucheintrag, ⁼e	*Sie macht einen Tagebucheintrag.*	*diary entry*

Lektion 21: Bei Rot musst du stehen, bei Grün darfst du gehen.

2

✓ der Autofahrer, -	Autofahrer bleiben bei Rot stehen.	motorist, car driver
✓ der Fahrradfahrer, -	Was machen Sie bei einer roten Ampel als Fahrradfahrer?	cyclist
✓ der Fußgänger, -	Als Fußgänger gehe ich manchmal bei Rot über die Ampel.	pedestrian
✓ stehen bleiben	Ich bleibe bei Rot immer stehen.	to stop
✓ *zu Fuß*	*Ich gehe oft zu Fuß.*	*to walk*

BILDLEXIKON

✓ angeln	*Mein Mann angelt gern.*	to go fishing
✓ baden	Im Sommer baden wir im Meer.	to swim
✓ erlauben	Ist Grillen im Park erlaubt?	to allow, to permit
✓ der Hund, -e	In vielen Geschäften sind Hunde verboten.	dog
✓ parken	Darf man hier parken?	to park
✓ das Picknick, -e und -s	Am Sonntag machen wir ein Picknick.	picnic
✓ reiten	*Kannst du reiten?*	to ride
✓ zelten	Wir zelten im Urlaub. Das ist günstig.	to camp

3

✓ der Helm, -e	*Warum müssen Fahrradfahrer keinen Helm tragen?*	*helmet*
✓ leise	In der Bibliothek muss man leise sein.	quiet
✓ der Mofafahrer, -	*Mofafahrer müssen einen Helm tragen.*	*moped rider*
✓ na schön	*Na schön, das kann man ja verstehen.*	*very well*
✓ regeln	Muss man wirklich alles regeln?	to regulate
✓ das Schild, -er	Sehen Sie die Schilder an.	sign, signpost
✓ tragen	Er trägt einen Helm auf dem Kopf.	to wear
✓ die Vermutung, -en	War Ihre Vermutung richtig?	assumption, supposition
✓ die Wiese, -n	Warum darf man nicht auf die Wiese gehen?	meadow, pasture

4

✓ an·legen	*Autofahrer müssen einen Gurt anlegen.*	*to put on*
✓ der Gurt, -e	*Bitte leg den Gurt an.*	*belt, seatbelt*
✓ hupen	In der Nähe von Krankenhäusern darf man nicht hupen.	to blow a horn, to honk
✓ das Krankenhaus, ⸚er	Im Krankenhaus muss man leise sein.	hospital
✓ der Motorradfahrer, -	Der Motorradfahrer fährt zu schnell.	motorcyclist, biker
✓ der Straßenverkehr (Sg.)	Im Straßenverkehr gibt es Regeln.	road transport

5

✓ gefährlich	Bei Rot über die Ampel gehen– das kann gefährlich sein.	dangerous

> **TIPP** Write short stories using the words from a chapter.

Mein Bruder ist im Krankenhaus. Ein Hund ist in sein Fahrrad gelaufen. Das war wirklich gefährlich ...

6

✓ die Leine, -n	*Hunde bitte an die Leine nehmen!*	*leash*
✓ schieben	Auf Parkwegen muss man das Fahrrad schieben.	to push
✓ verbieten	Eis essen ist im Bus verboten.	to prohibit, to forbid

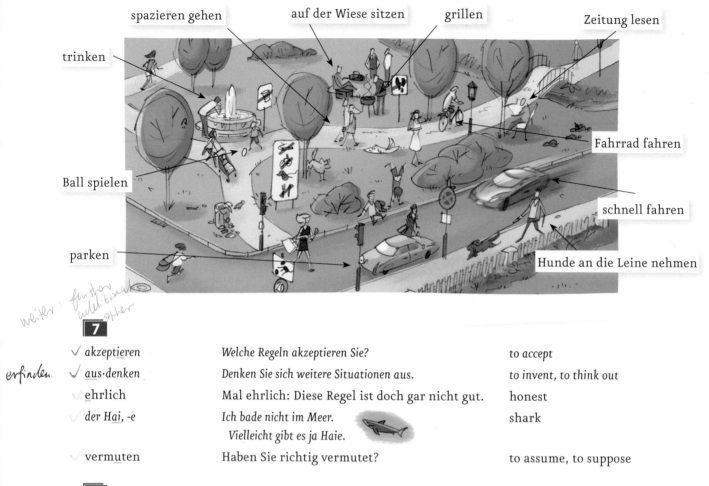

spazieren gehen · auf der Wiese sitzen · grillen · Zeitung lesen · trinken · Fahrrad fahren · Ball spielen · schnell fahren · parken · Hunde an die Leine nehmen

weiter: function additional other

7

erfinden

✓ akzeptieren	*Welche Regeln akzeptieren Sie?*	to accept
✓ aus·denken	*Denken Sie sich weitere Situationen aus.*	to invent, to think out
✓ ehrlich	Mal ehrlich: Diese Regel ist doch gar nicht gut.	honest
✓ der H<u>ai</u>, -e	*Ich bade nicht im Meer.* *Vielleicht gibt es ja Haie.*	shark
✓ verm<u>u</u>ten	Haben Sie richtig vermutet?	to assume, to suppose

8

✓ ab·stimmen	Stimmen Sie ab: In welcher Stadt möchten Sie leben?	to vote

LERNZIELE

✓ dürfen	Bei Rot darfst du nicht gehen.	may, to be allowed
✓ die M<u>ei</u>nung, -en	Sagen Sie Ihre Meinung.	<u>opinion</u>
✓ müssen	Du musst bei Rot stehen bleiben.	have to, to be obliged
✓ die R<u>e</u>gel, -n	Regeln, Regeln, Regeln – unser Leben ist voll mit Regeln.	rule
✓ schlimm	Das finde ich nicht so schlimm. *werfen throw*	bad, severe
✓ die Umwelt (Sg.)	Die Umwelt soll sauber bleiben! Werft Müll nicht auf die Straße.	<u>environment</u>
✓ *die Z<u>ei</u>tungskolumne, -n*	*Lesen Sie die Zeitungskolumne*	newspaper column

MODUL-PLUS LESEMAGAZIN

1

✓ die Arbeit, -en	*Ich komme gerade von der Arbeit.*	work
✓ *das Aufnahmegerät, -e*	*Ich schalte mein Aufnahmegerät ein.*	<u>recorder</u>

bloß	Junge, schlaf bloß nicht ein.	mere, just, only
dafür	Ich muss nur dreimal mitmachen, dafür bekomme ich auch noch Geld.	here: for it
der Dienstschluss (Sg.)	Heute habe ich um 13 Uhr Dienstschluss.	closing time, after-work
die Dienststelle, -n	Einmal im Jahr kommt mein Lieblingsfilm.	office
ein·checken	Am Nachmittag checke ich auf dem Schiff ein.	to check in
ein·schalten	= anmachen. Ich schalte mein Aufnahmegerät ein.	to switch on, to activate
ein·schlafen	Ich bin so müde. Hoffentlich schlafe ich nicht ein.	to fall asleep
das Europäische Magier- und Illusionisten- treffen, -	Ich soll auf dem Europäischen Magier- und Illusionisten- treffen meine neue Show vorstellen.	European magician and illusionist convention
der Fahrgast, ⸚e	Die meisten Fahrgäste sehen am Morgen noch sehr müde aus.	passenger
der Frühdienst, -e	Mein Frühdienst beginnt um sechs Uhr.	early duty/shift
halten: sauber halten	Man muss alles sauber halten.	to keep: to keep clean
herrlich	Die Arbeit auf dem Schiff ist wie Urlaub. Herrlich!	superb
die Karibik	Ich mache eine Fahrt in die Karibik.	Caribbean
kontrollieren	Bei meiner Arbeit muss man alles genau kontrollieren.	to check, to control
der Krankenpfleger, -	Adem arbeitet als Krankenpfleger.	male nurse
der Künstlername, -n	Der Künstlername von Markus Hirsch ist Argor Zafran.	screen name, stage name
legen	Adem muss die Patienten von einer Seite auf die andere legen.	to put
das Luxus-Schiff, -e	Die „Lady Amanda" ist ein Luxus-Schiff.	luxury vessel
das Messezentrum, -zentren	Um acht Uhr muss ich im Messezentrum sein.	exhibition centre
das Mikrofon, -e (das Mikro, -s)	Ich hole das Mikro aus der Tasche.	microphone
der Nachtdienst, -e	Der Nachtdienst beginnt um halb zehn Uhr abends.	night shift
der Nachtzug, ⸚e	Ich bin mit dem Nachtzug aus Rom gekommen.	night train, sleeper
normalerweise	Normalerweise beginnt der Dienst erst um halb acht.	normally, usually
der/die Operierte, -n	Die frisch Operierten muss man besonders genau kontrollieren.	patient who has been operated
der Pflegebericht, -e	Man muss Pflegeberichte schreiben.	care report
der Polizeibeamte, -n / die Polizeibeamtin, -nen	Marlies ist Polizeibeamtin.	police man/woman

✓ der Polizeiobermeister, - die Polizeiobermeisterin, -nen	Sie ist Polizeiobermeisterin.	police sergeant
✓ ruhig	Es ist ruhig in der U-Bahn.	quiet, calm
✓ die Schreibarbeit, -en	Als Polizistin hat man auch viel Schreibarbeit.	paperwork
✓ selbstständig	Markus Hirsch ist selbständig. Er arbeitet als Zauberer.	self-employed
✓ die Show, -s	Wie heißt die neue Show?	show
✓ das Showprogramm, -e	Ich mache dreimal im Showprogramm mit.	show programme
✓ der Spätdienst, -e	Die Kollegen vom Spätdienst wollen nach Hause.	late shift
✓ der Stadtteil, -e	Marlies ist mit einem Kollegen im Stadtteil unterwegs.	district
✓ der Streifendienst, -e	Im Streifendienst sind die Polizisten draußen.	patrol duty
✓ der U-Bahn-Waggon, -s	Am Morgen sind viele Fahrgäste im U-Bahn-Waggon.	subway carriage
✓ um·ziehen: sich um·ziehen	Ich ziehe mich auf der Wache um.	to get changed
✓ und so weiter	Man muss alles kontrollieren, alles sauber halten und so weiter.	and so on
✓ die Uniform, -en	Manche Kollegen kommen in Uniform zum Dienst.	uniform
✓ die Universitätsklinik, -en	Adem arbeitet in der Universitätsklinik.	university hospital
✓ die Wache, -n	Auf der Wache machen die Polizisten die Schreibarbeit.	here: police station
✓ der Zauberer, -	Argor Zafran ist ein Zauberer	magician, wizard

MODUL-PLUS FILM-STATIONEN

2

✓ die Generation, -en	Drei Generationen unter einem Dach – geht das gut?	generation
✓ miteinander	Wir leben gut miteinander.	together

3

✓ an·lehnen	Man darf hier kein Fahrrad anlehnen.	to lean (against)
✓ das Boot, -e	Boote sind hier verboten.	boat
✓ das Grundstück, -e	Man darf abends nicht auf das Grundstück gehen.	property
✓ der Musikclip, -s	Sehen Sie den Musikclip.	music clip
✓ das Surfbrett, -er	Boote und Surfbretter zu verkaufen	surfboard

MODUL-PLUS PROJEKT LANDESKUNDE

1

✓ der Animateur, -e	DJ Ötzi hat als Animateur gearbeitet.	host, holiday rep
✓ auf·wachsen (bei)	Er ist bei seiner Großmutter aufgewachsen.	to grow up (with)

die Augenfarbe, -n	Seine Augenfarbe ist braun.	eye colour
bürgerlich: bürgerlicher Name	Sein bürgerlicher Name ist Gerhard Friedle.	civil: civil name, real name
der Coversong, -s	Sein Coversong „Hey Babe" war ein Erfolg.	cover song
der DJ, -s	DJs arbeiten in Diskotheken, oder?	DJ
der Durchbruch, ⸚e	Sein Durchbruch folgt im Jahr 2000.	breakthrough
entdecken	Man hat DJ Ötzi bei einem Karaoke-Wettbewerb entdeckt.	to discover
der Entertainer, -	Er ist Entertainer und Musiker.	entertainer
färben	Seine Haare sind blond gefärbt.	to dye
folgen	Zuerst ist DJ Ötzi in den deutschsprachigen Ländern bekannt, dann folgt der internationale Durchbruch.	to follow
der Geburtsort, -e	Sein Geburtsort ist St. Johann in Tirol.	place of birth
die Haarfarbe, -n	Seine Haarfarbe ist blond, richtig?	hair colour
inzwischen	Inzwischen tragen auch viele Fans eine Mütze.	by now, in the meantime
der Karaoke-Wettbewerb, -e	Der Karaoke-Wettbewerb war der Start für eine Karriere als Musiker.	karaoke competition
der Koch, ⸚e	DJ Ötzi hat eine Ausbildung als Koch gemacht.	cook, chef
die Körpergröße (Sg.)	Seine Körpergröße: 1,83 m	body height
der Musikmanager, -	DJ Ötzis Frau ist die Musikmanagerin Sonja Kein.	music manager
das Porträt, -s	Lesen Sie das Porträt.	portrait
der Raum: im deutsch-sprachigen Raum	Zuerst war er nur im deutschsprachigen Raum bekannt.	area: in German speaking areas
der Schlagersänger, -	Der Schlagersänger wächst bei seiner Großmutter auf.	pop singer
selten	Nur selten sieht man ihn ohne Mütze.	rarely, seldom
die Strickmütze, -n	Man erkennt DJ Ötzi an seiner weißen Strickmütze.	knitted hat, beanie
(das) Tirol	Tirol ist in Österreich.	Tyrol
der Urlauber-Animateur, -e	Er ist als Urlauber-Animateur bekannt.	holiday host
die Welt, -en: zur Welt kommen	2002 ist seine Tochter zur Welt gekommen.	world: to be born (into the world)
weltweit	Weltweit hat der Sänger über 16 Millionen CDs verkauft.	worldwide
zunächst	Zunächst macht er eine Ausbildung als Koch, dann arbeitet er als Animateur.	initially

2

hängen (an)	Alle hängen ihre Fotos an eine Wand.	to hang (on)

1

ach nein!	*Ach nein, es tut mir leid, ich habe keine Zeit.*	oh no!
der Bitte-Danke-Walzer, -	*Wir tanzen den Bitte-Danke-Walzer.*	waltz dance (literally: Please-and-thank-you waltz)
frei: frei sein	Ist hier noch frei?	free: to be free
die Freude: Freude machen	Machen Sie mir doch die Freude.	joy, pleasure: to give sb. a treat
gern geschehen	*Dankeschön. – Bitte. Gern geschehen.*	my pleasure, you are welcome
der Ober, -	Herr Ober, wir möchten einen Tisch für zwei.	waiter
Oh!	*Oh, ein Walzer! Wie schön!*	oh!
der Platz: Nehmen Sie Platz.	Bitte, nehmen Sie Platz.	seat: take a seat
der Tanz, ⸚e	Schenken Sie mir diesen Tanz?	dance
verzeihen	Verzeihen Sie!	to pardon, to excuse
vorbei	Dürfen wir bitte vorbei?	past
der Walzer, -	*Können Sie Walzer tanzen?*	waltz

Lektion 19: Der hatte doch keinen Bauch!

Simple past tense Präteritum *of* sein *and* haben

Compound and simple past tenses exist in English and German. The rules however, when we use which tense, are very different.

The **Perfekt** tense is used in German **to speak** about the past. The simple past tense **Präteritum** is primarily used in **written** German.

Still few verbs are used **to speak** about the past in their **Präteritum** form, for example: **haben** and **sein**.

Walter **war** freundlich.   *Walter was friendly.*
Er **hatte** eine Brille.   *He had glasses.*

	sein	Präsens	Präteritum	**haben**	Präsens	Präteritum
ich	singular	bin	**war**	singular	habe	**hatte**
du		bist	**warst**		hast	**hattest**
er/es/sie		ist	**war**		hat	**hatte**
wir	plural	sind	**waren**	plural	haben	**hatten**
ihr		seid	**wart**		habt	**hattet**
sie/Sie		sind	**waren**		haben	**hatten**

In Präteritum, **the first** and **the third** person singular are always **identical**. Also most irregular verbs have **no specific ending** (just the principal form) in **the first** and **the third** person singular.

Perfekt (the compound past tense) of inseparable verbs

The **inseparable verbs** form the past participle **without ge-** in front; it doesn't matter if the verb is regular or not. At the end of the participle the regular verbs get an ending **-t** and the irregular verbs mostly **-en**.

These prefixes are always inseparable:

be-
bekommen → bekommen
Maria **hat** ein Baby **bekommen**.   *Maria had a baby.*

er-
erkennen → erkannt
Tom **hat** Anna gleich **erkannt**.   *Mark recognized Anna immediately.*

ent-
sich entschuldigen → entschuldigt
Er **hat** sich **entschuldigt**.   *He apologized.*

Grammar Explanations

ge-
gefallen → gefallen
Mark **hat** mir nicht **gefallen**.   *I didn't like Mark.*

ver-
vergessen → vergessen
Ich **habe** meine Tasche **vergessen**.   *I forgot my bag.*

Word forming with un-

Un- is a prefix that can be combined with many adjectives, forming the opposite meaning (often negative – but not always!)

glücklich ↔ **un**glücklich – *happy ↔ unhappy*
interessant ↔ **un**interessant – *interesting ↔ uninteresting*

Expressing surprise

Reacting to news or gossip, it might be useful to know, how to express surprise:

Information:
→ Brad Pitt ist wieder Single!   *Brad Pitt is single again!*

Possible reactions that will express surprise:
→ Ach du liebe Zeit!   *Dear me!*
→ Ach komm!   *No kidding!*
→ Ach was!   *No kidding!*
→ Echt?   *Really?*
→ Wahnsinn!   *Awesome!*

Lektion 20: Komm sofort runter!

Imperative forms of du and ihr   *(no umlaut for du) -*

The imperative mood is used to express **a command or a plea**, sometimes a **suggestion**. The speaker is addressing someone directly. The imperative can be formed for the second person singular **du**, second person plural **ihr** and the **Sie**-person.

The imperative for the second person singular **du** is formed from the verb's conjugated form, but used without the person and the ending:

machen → ~~du~~ **mach**st → **Mach** dein Bett! *Make your bed!*

vergessen → ~~du~~ **vergiss**t → **Vergiss** deine Hausaufgaben nicht! *Don't forget your homework!*

ausräumen → ~~du~~ **räum**st **aus** → **Räum** die Spülmaschine **aus**! *Empty the dishwasher!*

② The imperative for the second person plural **ihr** is formed from the verb's conjugated form, but used without the person:

machen → ~~ihr~~ **macht** → **Macht** eure Betten!   *Make your beds!*

vergessen → ~~ihr~~ **vergesst** → **Vergesst** eure Hausaufgaben nicht!
 Don't forget your homework!

ausräumen → ~~ihr~~ **räumt aus** → **Räumt** die Spülmaschine **aus**!   *Empty the dishwasher!*

Imperative of sein and haben

The verbs **sein** and **haben** don't follow the rules for forming **the second person singular**. Their imperative forms have to be memorized. Plural forms follow the rules.

sein → conjugated form: **du bist** → imperative form:
 Sei → **Sei** nicht so faul!   *Don't be so lazy!*

haben → conjugated form: **du hast** → imperative form:
 Hab! → **Hab** keine Angst!   *Don't be afraid!*

Imperative filling words mal, doch and bitte

Imperative sentences can sound very bossy and impolite. Filling words **bitte, mal** or **doch** are very useful, in order to make the command or request sound more polite and friendly (even if it is not always visible in English translation):

Spül **bitte** das Geschirr!   *Wash the dishes, please!*
Ruf ihn **doch** zurück!   *Call him back!*
Warte **mal**!   *Wait for me!*

Personal pronouns in accusative case

The nouns in the accusative case can be replaced by pronouns:

Das Bad war sehr schmutzig.   **The bathroom** *was dirty.*
 Ich habe **es** geputzt.   *I cleaned **it** quickly.*

Personal pronouns in the accusative case can also be intended objects:
Kannst du **mich** abholen?   *Can you pick **me** up?*

	personal pronoun					
nominative	ich	du	er/es/sie	wir	ihr	sie/Sie
accusative	mich	dich	ihn/es/sie	uns	euch	sie/Sie

Grammar Explanations

Lektion 21: Bei Rot musst du stehen, bei Grün darfst du gehen.

Confusing words: mein/e, meinen, Meinung

These words can become confusing, especially if close to each other:

mein/e (*my*) → possessive pronoun
Ich besuche **meine** Tante und **meinen** Onkel gern.   *I like visiting my aunt and uncle.*

meinen (*to think, to mean sth.*) → verb
Ich finde das Bild schön und was **meinen** Sie?   *I like the picture and what do you think?*

die Meinung (*opinion*) → noun
Wie ist Ihre **Meinung** dazu?   *What is your opinion about it?*

Example of all three in one sentence:
Das ist **meine Meinung** und was **meinen** Sie dazu?   *That's my opinion and what do you think?*

Modal auxiliary müssen

The verb **müssen** is one of the modal auxiliaries (Modalverben) and it is used to express the things that we **must** do / **have to** do.

Like other modal auxiliaries in German the verb **müssen** is often used with the **infinitive** of other verbs. The infinitive is placed at the end of the sentence and builds **the sentence bracket**.

Du **musst** in der Bibliothek leise **sein**.   *You **have to be** quiet in the library.*
Motorradfahrer **müssen** einen Helm **tragen**.   *Motor bikers **must wear** helmets.*

		müssen
singular	ich	**muss**
	du	**musst**
	er/sie	**muss**
plural	wir	müssen
	ihr	müsst
	sie/Sie	müssen

Modal auxiliary dürfen

The verb **dürfen** is one of the modal auxiliaries (Modalverben) and is used to express the things that we are allowed or even more often not allowed to / must not do.

Like other modal auxiliaries in German the verb **dürfen** is often used with the **infinitive** of other verbs. The infinitive is placed at the end of the sentence and builds **the sentence bracket**.

Du **darfst** keine Schokolade **essen**.
Man **darf** hier **nicht parken**.

You're **not allowed to eat** chocolate.
One **must not park** here.

		dürfen
singular	ich	**darf**
	du	**darfst**
	er/sie	**darf**
plural	wir	dürfen
	ihr	dürft
	sie/Sie	dürfen

Problems with nicht müssen and nicht dürfen

English speakers have a natural tendency to understand „muss nicht" as "must not", which is not correct.

The sentence: „Ich **muss nicht** arbeiten." does **NOT** mean "I must not work.", but "I **don't have to** work."

"I must not **work**." is in German: „**Ich darf nicht arbeiten**."

Therefore it's easier to understand and translate the modal auxiliary **müssen** as "**have to**" than "must".

Irregular verb tragen

The verb **tragen** (to carry or to wear) is irregular and has a vowel change **a → ä**.

		tragen
singular	ich	trage
	du	trägst
	er/sie	trägt
plural	wir	tragen
	ihr	tragt
	sie/Sie	tragen

Der Fahrradfahrer **trägt** keinen Helm.   *The biker doesn't wear a helmet.*

Cultural Studies

Haben Sie Punkte in Flensburg?

Talking about long German words, the following one has to join the list – *Kraftfahrzeug-bundesamt (short KBA)*. The meaning is Federal Motor Transport Authority and it is an important institution for all German drivers as it deals with road safety, information on road traffic and environmental protection.

The KBA is based in the city of Flensburg in the north of Schleswig-Holstein close to the Danish border. One body of the *Kraftfahrzeugbundesamt* is the Central Register of Traffic Offenders which deals with the penalty points system. So Flensburg is especially famous for this database of traffic violators – the traffic-sinner file. Major traffic offences and violations are allotted points in the Central Register of Traffic Offenders, with a higher number of points given for the more severe offences, as well as a fine. Once a driver has reached 18 points or more, their driving permit is withdrawn and they are not allowed to drive for a period of time. So when you hear Germans talking about having *Punkte in Flensburg* (points in Flensburg), you know what they are referring to.

Things to know when you are on the road...

The German *Autobahn* is famous for having no official maximum speed limit. Drivers are trusted to drive at the fastest safe speed for their particular car. Considering Germany is home to BMW, Audi and Mercedes – all widely recognised for their fast sports cars – the Germans do drive quickly. Drivers who drive more economical cars will be pleased to know that the recommended speed limit is a moderate 130 km/h.

In reality, driving incredibly fast in sports cars is not possible everywhere due to the weather, road works, peak hour speed limits and general road traffic.

Germany has two significant transit routes for road freight: the north-south and east-west axis, so there is a high volume of freight trucks. These commercial trucks are charged a toll and are subject to strict weight restrictions which are frequently monitored.

Before driving on Austrian Motorways, you are obliged to purchase an Austrian Motorway Tax Ticket called a Vignette, or as the Austrians say a *Pickerl* (literally meaning 'sticker'), which is commonly available in roadside services. They can be purchased for the periods – 10 days, 2 months or a full calendar year, and are a must when driving on

Austrian Motorways. Failing to display a valid and properly-secured Vignette will lead to an on-the-spot charge of 120 euro to 240 euro, which rises steeply to 300 euro to 3000 euro when administration and court costs are automatically included.

The maximum speed limit is 130 km/h on motorways. However, many sections have a lower or variable speed limit for safety reasons, for example mountain passes that are prone to severe weather.

Winter equipment is mandatory between 1ˢᵗ of November and 15ᵗʰ of April which means that the car must either be fitted with four winter tyres or it has to have two snow chains on at least two tyres. This is on top of the year-round requirement to carry high visibility vests, a first aid kit and warning triangle. So make sure you have all these on board when driving in Austria as the fines are very expensive.

On the subject of expensive fines, it is well known that fines for violating traffic regulations are very high in Switzerland and Swiss police in particular are notorious for issuing fines for the smallest of offences.

There is an annual motorway tax in Switzerland that must be paid even if you need to use a motorway for a very short period of time. Actually, it is almost considered mandatory for all drivers, as being a transit country, it is difficult to avoid a motorway, even on the shortest of trips. Also, the Swiss road infrastructure is well advanced and motorways are incredibly common. The national maximum speed limit is 120 km/h.

Nations of Rubbish Sorters

If you ever want to live in a German speaking country, be prepared to recycle almost everything as these are the countries with the highest recycling rates in the world. Germany is regarded as a highly established recycling country and for the past few years Germany, Austria and Belgium have been named top recycling countries in Europe. In fact, Austria is said to lead the way in Europe with over 70% of waste either recycled or composted.

So are they all doing it? Statistics suggest that on average greater than two thirds of the population are actively recycling. That is quite a significant majority but with 30% still not properly sorting their rubbish, there is still room for improvement. Due to the small minority that don't follow the system, the question often arises whether automatic sorting machines should be employed instead. However, so far they have kept the current, manual system in place.

And what is the secret to success in these countries? There are various strategies. All stores add a small deposit to particular reusable plastic and glass bottle as well as some drinking cans with a *Pfand* (deposit) symbol. On returning them back to the store, the customer receives a refund and the bottles are returned to the producer for reuse. *The act of taking one's empty Pfand bottles to the supermarket has simply become a habit for many and it will add to a significant amount after even a short period of time.* The remaining glass is separated into colour groups – white, brown and green, before being recycled in special

das Pfand (Pfänder)

bins. These bins can be found in many locations around town, but please do remember not to use them during quiet time as it is considered being too noisy. *Ruhezeit* (quiet time) is from 10 p.m. to 6 a.m., all day on a Sunday, on public holidays and furthermore in some regions also between 1 p.m. and 3 p.m. each weekday.

Next on the list is paper, cardboard, newspapers, magazines, paper bags etc. Naturally, they are also collected and each goes into a separate bin. Please note that paper tissues do not belong in these bins.

Used packaging featuring the green dot symbol (*Grüner Punkt*) which is made of metal, natural materials, plastic and composites belong in the yellow bin or the yellow sack and get collected fortnightly or every couple of weeks depending on location.

Garden waste and food scraps are generally disposed in a brown bin and get emptied very regularly – especially in summer. Batteries are collected separately in small bins which can be found in most shops and stores. Metal scrap is collected, sorted and either reused or recycled. Hazardous waste is disposed of properly too, generally only a couple of times per year – depending on location. A notice from the council is sent to individual households to let people know when and where they can discard their dangerous waste.

And can you believe that even clothes and shoes are collected at clothes and shoe banks which are generally run by private companies or charities for reuse or recycling! Bigger items such as old broken furniture and electrical appliances can be taken to the *Recyclinghof*, a recycling yard especially for hard rubbish. Easy!

The remaining waste can simply be placed in the black garbage bin, but as you may have noticed there is usually not much left!

On that note: happy sorting!

Lektion 22: Am besten sind seine Schuhe!

1

✓ die Reaktion, -en	Wie findet Fabian die Reaktion seiner Mutter?	reaction

BILDLEXIKON

✓ die Bluse, -n	Was kaufst du nie? – Blusen! Ich bin doch keine Frau.	blouse
✓ der Gürtel, -	*Der Gürtel ist aus Leder.* leather (das, -).	belt
✓ der Hut, ⸚e	*Ich habe noch nie einen Hut gekauft.*	hat
✓ die Jacke, -n	Meine Jacke ist braun.	coat, jacket
✓ das Kleid, -er	Veras Kleid gefällt mir besser als Jasmins Kleid.	dress
✓ der Mantel, ⸚	Dein Mantel gefällt mir.	coat
✓ der Pullover, -	Wie gefällt dir der Pullover?	jumper, sweater
✓ der Rock, ⸚e	Ich kaufe oft Röcke. Ich liebe Röcke.	skirt
✓ die Socke, -n	Weiße Socken zu schwarzen Schuhen? – Schlimm. bad	sock
✓ der Strumpf, ⸚e	Ein blauer und ein roter Strumpf. Wie lustig!	stocking
✓ die Strumpfhose, -n	Ich brauche eine Strumpfhose. Haben Sie Strumpfhosen?	tights (pl.)

> **TIPP** Cut out images and add the words for the outfit.

2

✓ an·haben	Meine Person hat eine Hose und einen Pullover an.	to wear
✓ das Ratespiel, -e	Ratespiel: Was hat die Person an?	guessing game

3

✓ beige	*Die Hose ist beige.*	●	*beige*
✓ golden	*Seine Schuhe sind golden.*	●	*golden*
✓ das Kostüm, -e	Toll! Ein super Kostüm hast du an.		costume
✓ lila	*Ein lila Hemd? Nein, das mag ich nicht.*	●	*purple*
✓ rosa	*Rosa ist meine Lieblingsfarbe.*	●	*pink*

Hut — Jacke — Gürtel — Kleid — Strumpfhose — Schuhe

Mütze — Hemd — Mantel — Pullover — Hose

4

✓ genauso … wie	Elena mag Lila genauso gern wie Rosa.	just as

5

✓ das Forum, Foren	Lesen Sie die Texte im Forum.	forum
✓ Klasse!	Klasse, Fred! Das Foto ist cool.	here: excellent, terrific
✓ klug	Marco ist klüger als alle anderen.	smart
✓ das Lieblings-T-Shirt, -s	Ich habe nicht nur ein Lieblings-T-Shirt.	favourite T-shirt
✓ schauen	Schau mal, dieses T-Shirt ist noch lustiger.	to look
✓ tragen: einen Rock tragen	Trägst du oft Röcke und Kleider?	to wear: to wear a skirt
✓ ziemlich	Mein T-Shirt ist schon ziemlich alt.	fairly

6

eigen: own, separate, typical

✓ entwerfen	*Entwerfen Sie Ihr eigenes T-Shirt.*	to design

7

✓ das Lieblings-Kleidungsstück, -e	Beschreiben Sie Ihr Lieblings-Kleidungsstück.	favourite piece of clothing
✓ an·ziehen (sich)	Wann hast du dein Lieblings-T-Shirt zuletzt angezogen?	to put on
✓ die Band, -s	*Ich höre die Band „Mondschein" gern.*	band
✓ das Kleidungsstück, -e	Was gefällt dir an dem Kleidungsstück am besten?	item of clothing, garment
✓ zuletzt	Ich ziehe das T-Shirt oft an, zuletzt am Montag.	last

in the end

8

✓ die Betonung, -en	*Achten Sie auf die Betonung!*	emphasis, stress
✓ der Katalog, -e	*Sehen Sie in einen Katalog.*	catalogue
✓ Seht mal!	*Seht mal, das Kleid ist richtig toll.*	Look!
✓ Wow!	*Wow, hast du das Kleid gesehen?*	Wow!
✓ die Zeitschrift, -en	Lesen Sie gern Zeitschriften?	magazine

LERNZIELE

✓ der Forumsbeitrag, ⸚e	Lesen Sie die Forumsbeiträge.	forum post
✓ das Hemd, -en	Das Hemd gefällt ihr.	shirt
✓ die Hose, -n	Das Hemd gefällt ihr besser als die Hose.	trousers (pl.)
✓ die Komparation, -en	*Komparation: gut, besser, am besten*	comparison
✓ der Schuh, -e	Am besten sind seine Schuhe!	shoe
✓ der Vergleich, -e	Vergleich: Die Hose gefällt ihr. Aber das Hemd gefällt ihr besser als die Hose.	comparison
✓ verstärken	*Aussagen verstärken: Total schön.*	to reinforce, to strengthen

GRAMMATIK & KOMMUNIKATION

✓ der Komparativ, -e	Komparativ-Formen: besser, lieber …	comparative degree
✓ der Positiv, -e	Positiv-Formen: gut, gern …	positive degree
✓ der Superlativ, -e	Superlativ-Formen: am besten, liebsten …	superlative degree

Lektion 23: Ins Wasser gefallen?

1

✓ die Laune, -n	Laura hat schlechte Laune.	mood

2

✓ gleich	Es geht mir gleich viel besser.	in a bit
✓ der Milchkaffee, -s	Im Café trinke ich immer Milchkaffee.	latte, milky coffee

BILDLEXIKON

✓ das Gewitter, -	Hast du Angst vor Gewitter?	thunderstorm
✓ das Grad, -e	Wie viel Grad sind es heute?	degree
✓ kühl	Es ist kühl, nur acht Grad.	chilly, cool
✓ minus	Bei minus 20 Grad gehe ich nicht aus dem Haus.	minus
✓ der Nebel, -	Gibt es in Hamburg viel Nebel?	fog
✓ der Schnee (Sg.)	Ich liebe Schnee und Skifahren.	snow
✓ warm	Es ist warm, denn es ist Sommer.	warm
✓ der Wind, -e	Fünf Tage lang kein bisschen Wind – und das am Meer.	wind
✓ die Wolke, -n	Am Himmel sind weiße Wolken zu sehen.	cloud

die Sonne / Es ist sonnig.

der Schnee / Es schneit.

der Nebel / Es ist neblig.

der Regen / Es regnet.

der Wind / Es ist windig.

die Wolke / Es ist bewölkt.

das Gewitter / Es blitzt und donnert.

WETTER

TIPP Look for word families.

Wolke — bewölkt — wolkenlos
Reise — Reiseführer — reisen — Reisebüro

3

✓ blitzen	Bei Gewitter blitzt es.	to flash, lightning
✓ donnern	Es donnert.	to thunder
✓ neblig	Es ist neblig.	foggy
✓ schneien	Im Winter schneit es in den Bergen.	to snow
✓ sonnig	Es ist sonnig.	sunny
✓ windig	*Es ist windig.*	*windy*

der Norden

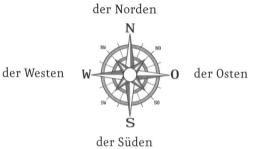

der Westen   der Osten

der Süden

4

✓ auf·wachen	Letzten Sonntag bin ich um sechs Uhr aufgewacht.	to wake up
✓ bis zu	*Es kann bis zu zwei Grad werden.*	up to, till
✓ brauchbar	*Wir hatten einen Reiseführer mit brauchbaren Tipps dabei.*	convenient, suitable
✓ der Campingstuhl, ⸚e	Bis zum späten Nachmittag haben wir auf unseren Campingstühlen gesessen.	camping chair
✓ (dabei·haben)	Hast du eine Regenjacke dabei? Es regnet.	to carry along
✓ das Dach, ⸚er	Unsere Zimmer waren ganz oben, direkt unter dem Dach.	roof
✓ ein paar	Leider waren wir nur ein paar Stunden in der Wohnung.	a few
✓ erleben	Hast du so etwas schon einmal erlebt?	to experience
✓ farblos	*Alles war grau und farblos.*	colourless
✓ die Ferienwohnung, -en	Die Ferienwohnung war toll.	holiday apartment
✓ das Frühjahr, -e	= Frühling	spring
✓ furchtbar	Das Unwetter war furchtbar.	terrible
✓ genug	Da sind wir wohl nicht weit genug in den Süden gefahren.	enough
✓ die Geschwindigkeit, -en	Der Sturm hatte bis zu 160 km/h Geschwindigkeit.	speed, velocity
✓ hart	Der Winter war lang und hart.	severe, hard
✓ das Hausdach, ⸚er	Das Hausdach war nach dem Sturm kaputt.	rooftop
✓ der Himmel, -	Der Himmel ist blau, das Wetter ist gut.	sky
✓ km/h (Stundenkilometer)	*Wie schnell fährt dein Auto? – 200 km/h.*	kilometer per hour

der Kurzurlaub, -e	Es war nur ein Kurzurlaub, aber es war wunderbar.	mini-break
mit·machen	Mach mit und schick mir deinen Text.	to participate, to join in
das Mittelmeer	Nächstes Jahr fahren wir ans Mittelmeer.	Mediterranean
der Neuschnee (Sg.)	Heute Nacht hat es geschneit: 10 cm Neuschnee.	fresh snow
der Norden (Sg.)	Fahren Sie Richtung Norden.	north
öffnen	Ich öffne die Tür und sehe: Es hat geschneit.	to open
der Osten (Sg.)	Wir wohnen im Osten von Berlin.	east
die Ostsee	Letztes Jahr sind wir an die Ostsee gefahren.	Baltic Sea
das Pech	Wir hatten leider Pech: nur Regen und Nebel.	here: misfortune
der Problemurlaub, -e	In diesem Blog sammle ich Texte über Problemurlaube.	holiday problem
der Problemurlaubs-Blog, -s	Sandra hat einen Problemurlaubs-Blog.	blog about holiday problems
der Reiseführer, -	In diesem Reiseführer sind gute Tipps.	here: guidebook; also: tour guide
scheinen	Die Sonne scheint.	to shine
der Schwarzwald	Wo liegt der Schwarzwald?	Black Forest
sitzen	Das Wetter ist herrlich, wir sitzen den ganzen Tag in der Sonne.	to sit
der Sommerurlaub, -e	Unser Sommerurlaub war perfekt.	summer holiday
der Sturm, ⁻e	Ein Sturm kann gefährlich sein.	storm
der Süden (Sg.)	Wir fahren in den Süden.	south
(das) Südtirol	Südtirol liegt in Italien.	South Tyrol
der Super-Badestrand, ⁻e	Urlaubsfotos vom Super-Badestrand möchten wir nicht sehen.	super beach
die Temperatur, -en	Wir hatten einen Traumurlaub bei Temperaturen zwischen 18 und 22 Grad.	temperature
Tja!	Tja, da müssen wir nächstes Mal besser in den Süden fahren.	oh well!
der Traum, ⁻e	Unser Urlaub ist ein Traum!	dream
das Traumwetter (Sg.)	Wir hatten Traumwetter.	dream weather
unglaublich	Der Urlaub war unglaublich.	unbelievable
das Unwetter, -	Dann ist das Unwetter gekommen.	storm, tempest
das Urlaubsfoto, -s	Schick mir doch ein paar Urlaubsfotos.	holiday pictures
der Westen (Sg.)	Im Westen sind es 20 Grad.	west
das Wohnmobil, -e	Wir sind mit dem Wohnmobil nach Südtirol gefahren.	camper van
wolkenlos	Der Himmel ist wolkenlos.	cloudless
wunderbar	Alles war wunderbar: das Wetter, das Essen, die Leute.	wonderful
das Ziel, -e	Unser Ziel war Südtirol.	destination

5

✓ begründen	= einen Grund angeben	to justify
✓ der Kinofilm, -e	Malte liebt Kinofilme.	film, motion picture
✓ die Spalte, -n	Ergänzen Sie Ihre Spalte.	column

6

✓ das Lieblingswetter, -	Mein Lieblingswetter? Nicht zu warm, ein bisschen Wind und Sonne.	favourite weather
✓ die Melodie, Melodien	Welche Melodie gefällt Ihnen am besten?	melody
✓ der Rhythmus, Rhythmen	Bei diesem Rhythmus denke ich an mein Lieblingswetter.	rhythm
✓ die Wetterassoziation, -en	Hören Sie. Welche Wetterassoziationen haben Sie?	association to the weather

7

✓ bis bald	Tschüs, bis bald!	see you soon
✓ groß·schreiben	Haben Sie alle Nomen großgeschrieben?	to capitalize
✓ (das) Kreta	Wir sind gerade auf Kreta.	Crete
✓ das Leben, -	So ist das Leben wunderbar.	life

LERNZIELE

✓ an·geben	Warum können Sie nicht kommen? Geben Sie einen Grund an.	to state sth.
✓ bewölkt	Es ist bewölkt.	cloudy
✓ denn (Konjunktion)	Gründe kann man mit denn angeben.	here: because
✓ der Grund, ¨e	Was ist der Grund für deine schlechte Laune?	reason
✓ die Himmelsrichtung, -en	Die Kinder laufen in alle Himmelsrichtungen.	cardinal direction
✓ die Konjunktion, -en	denn ist eine Konjunktion.	conjunction

Lektion 24: Ich würde am liebsten jeden Tag feiern.

1

✓ bestehen	Isabella hat die Prüfung bestanden.	to pass
✓ die Überraschungsparty, -s	Wir machen eine Überraschungsparty für Isabella.	surprise party

BILDLEXIKON

✓ die Einweihungsparty, -s	Die Einweihungsparty ist in zwei Wochen.	housewarming party
✓ das Ostern, -	Was macht ihr Ostern?	Easter
✓ das Weihnachten, -	Weiße Weihnachten – ein Traum!	Christmas

Weihnachten

Ostern

Silvester/Neujahr

Geburtstag

FESTE

Hochzeit

Einweihungsparty

Karneval

Prüfung bestanden

2

√ abends	Hast du am 4. Mai abends Zeit?	in the evening
√ die Abschlussprüfung, -en	Hast du die Abschlussprüfung schon gemacht?	*final examination*
Boah!	*30 Jahre? Boah!*	*oh wow!*
√ entspannen (sich)	*Du musst dich mehr entspannen.*	to relax
√ die Fitness (Sg.)	Du musst mehr für die Fitness tun.	fitness
√ das Fitnessstudio, -s	Kommst du mit ins Fitnessstudio?	gym, fitness studio
√ das Getränk, -e	Wer bringt Getränke mit?	drink
√ der Gutschein, -e	Ich habe zum Geburtstag einen Gutschein für das Fitnessstudio bekommen.	*voucher*
√ die Hantel, -n	Im Fitnesskurs benutzen wir Hanteln.	*dumbbell*
√ die Hauseinweihungs-party, -s	Wir machen eine Hauseinweihungsparty.	*housewarming party*
der Heilige Abend (Sg.)	Der Heilige Abend ist am 24. Dezember.	*Christmas Eve*
√ hoffentlich	Hoffentlich kannst du zur Party kommen.	hopefully
der Kinogutschein, -e	Wir schenken ihm einen Kinogutschein.	cinema voucher
√ der Papa, -s	Was schenken wir Papa?	dad
√ zufrieden	Wir sind glücklich und zufrieden mit dem Haus.	satisfied, content

3

√ das Lieblingsfest, -e	Was ist dein Lieblingsfest?	*favourite celebration*

4

√ die CD, -s	Konzerte sind immer besser als CDs.	CD
√ der Glückwunsch, ⁻e	Welches Fest passt zu den Glückwünschen?	congratulation
√ das Konzertticket, -s	Ich bekomme am liebsten Konzerttickets.	concert ticket

7

√ der / die Bekannte, -n	Wir feiern Silvester mit Bekannten.	acquaintance, friend
√ draußen	Das Wetter ist schön. Wir können draußen feiern.	outside
√ das Feuerwerk, -e	Ich mag Feuerwerke nicht. 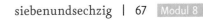	*firework*

✓ der Sekt, -e	Ich darf keinen Sekt trinken, ich muss noch Auto fahren.	sparkling wine
✓ der/die Verwandte, -n	Alle Verwandten und Freunde sind zur Einweihungsparty gekommen.	relative

LERNZIELE

✓ Herzlichen Glückwunsch	Herzlichen Glückwunsch zum Geburtstag.	congratulations, best wishes
der Konjunktiv II, -e	Konjunktiv II: Das würde ich am liebsten jeden Tag machen.	subjunctive
✓ die Ordinalzahl, -en	Was sind Ordinalzahlen? – Der erste, zweite …	ordinal number

GRAMMATIK & KOMMUNIKATION

✓ das Datum, Daten	Welches Datum ist morgen?	date

MODUL-PLUS LESEMAGAZIN

1

✓ befürchten	Der Klimawandel ist stärker als wir befürchtet haben.	to fear
✓ die Chefsekretärin, -nen	Sonja Zimmerer arbeitet als Chefsekretärin.	chief secretary, PA
✓ die Daten (Pl.)	Es gibt viele Daten über den Klimawandel.	data, facts
✓ das Diagramm, -e	Das Diagramm zeigt einen Zeitraum von 125 Jahren.	graph, diagram
✓ die Eiszeit (Sg.)	Wann war die Eiszeit?	Ice age
✓ heiß	Es war mal heißer und mal kälter.	hot
✓ jedenfalls	Ich habe jedenfalls keine Angst vor dem Klimawandel.	anyway, in any rate
✓ das Klima (Sg.)	Viele machen sich Sorgen um das Klima.	climate
✓ die Klimaveränderung, -en	Die Klimaveränderung ist eine Tatsache.	climate change
✓ der Klimawandel (Sg.)	Der Klimawandel kommt sehr schnell.	climate change
✓ der Planet, -en	Das Klima auf unserem Planeten verändert sich.	planet
✓ die Politik (Sg.)	Es geht hier um Politik und Geld.	politics
✓ die Politikwissenschaft, -en	Arwed studiert Politikwissenschaften.	political science
✓ regnen	Früher hat es mehr geregnet.	to rain
✓ die Sorge, -n: (sich Sorgen machen)	Die meisten Menschen machen sich Sorgen ums Klima.	worry: to worry about sth.
das Speditionsunternehmen, -	Was macht ein Speditionsunternehmen?	truck company, shipping company
✓ die Tatsache, -n	Das ist eine Tatsache!	fact
✓ unterschiedlich	Unterschiedliche Temperaturen sind normal.	different
✓ verändern	Wir müssen unser Leben verändern.	to change
✓ vergangen	Wir dürfen nicht weiterleben wie in den vergangenen Jahren.	past
✓ weiter·leben	Wir können so weiterleben wie immer.	to continue to live

✓ wenig	Ein Diagramm sagt wenig, findet Sonja.	little
✓ die Wissenschaft, -en	Es geht beim Klimawandel nicht um Wissenschaft.	science
✓ der Zeitraum, ⸚e	*In dem Diagramm geht es um den Zeitraum von 1890 bis 2005.*	*period, timeframe*
✓ der Zufall, ⸚e	Das kann doch kein Zufall sein!	coincidence

MODUL-PLUS FILM-STATIONEN

1

✓ die Modenschau, -en	*Sehen Sie die Modenschau.*	*fashion show*
✓ passen	*Das Kleid passt zu dir.*	*to suit*

2

✓ der Aussichtsturm, ⸚e	Auf dem Aussichtsturm hat man einen schönen Blick auf Bern.	viewing tower
✓ die Sicht (Sg.)	*Die Sicht ist schlecht, denn es ist neblig.*	*view*

3

✓ der Autoscooter, -	*Ich will Autoscooter fahren.*	*bumper car*
✓ gucken	*Guck mal, da sind Autoscooter.*	*to watch*
✓ der Jahrmarkt, ⸚e	*Die Auer Dult ist ein bekannter Jahrmarkt.*	*fair*
✓ schießen	*Schießt du auf dem Jahrmarkt eine Blume für mich?*	*to shoot*

MODUL-PLUS PROJEKT LANDESKUNDE

1

✓ auf·stellen	*Im Sommer stellen wir im Garten die Liegestühle auf.*	*to establish, to arrange*
✓ der Badeanzug, ⸚e	Zur Strandparty kommen alle im Badeanzug.	swimsuit
✓ die Badehose, -n	Männer tragen eine Badehose.	swimming trunks (pl.)
✓ bestimmt-	Wir wollen eine Party zu einem bestimmten Thema feiern.	certain
✓ der Bikini, -s	*Der Bikini ist sehr schön.*	*bikini*
✓ die Dekoration, -en	Luftballons sind wichtig für die Dekoration.	decoration
✓ dekorieren	Wir dekorieren den Raum mit Sand.	to decorate
✓ exotisch	*Essen und Getränke sollten exotisch sein.*	*exotic*
✓ das Fischbuffet, -s	Ein Fischbuffet kostet nicht viel.	fish buffet
✓ die Flaschenpost (Sg.)	Wir haben im Urlaub eine Flaschenpost geschickt.	letter in a bottle
✓ der Fruchtcocktail, -s	*Möchtest du einen Fruchtcocktail?*	*fruit cocktail*
✓ jedem	Fruchtcocktails schmecken jedem.	anyone whom (dative)
✓ der Liegestuhl, ⸚e	Im Urlaub liegt Mama nur im Liegestuhl.	deckchair

✓ das Luftballon-Darts (Sg.)	Ein Luftballon-Darts ist das perfekte Spiel für Strand-Partys.	balloon darts
✓ das Motto, -s	Wählen Sie ein Motto für Ihre Party.	slogan
✓ die Motto-Party, -s	Eine Motto-Party ist eine Party zu einem bestimmten Thema.	theme party
✓ der Party-Raum, ⸚e	Wer dekoriert den Party-Raum?	party room
✓ das Planschbecken, -	Ein Planschbecken darf an heißen Tagen nicht fehlen.	paddling pool
✓ das Programm, -e	Was wäre eine Party ohne Programm?	programme
✓ der Raum, ⸚e	Wie sieht der Raum aus?	room
✓ der Sand, -e	Am Strand gibt es viel Sand.	sand
✓ sorgen (für)	Wer sorgt für die Getränke?	to care (for)
✓ der Spielvorschlag, ⸚e	Hast du einen Spielvorschlag für die Party?	suggestion for a game
✓ die Stimmung, -en	Salsa-Musik sorgt für eine tolle Stimmung.	atmosphere
✓ die Strand-Motto-Party, -s	Auf einer Strand-Motto-Party passen Bikini und Badehose am besten.	beach themed party
✓ die Strand-Party, -s	Wir feiern eine Strand-Party.	beach party
✓ der Themenvorschlag, ⸚e	Auf dieser Seite findet ihr viele Themen-vorschläge.	suggestion for a topic
✓ der Toast Hawaii	Hast du schon einmal Toast Hawaii gegessen?	toast hawaii
✓ der Umschlag, ⸚e	Wir stecken den Brief in den Umschlag.	envelope
✓ vorbei·bringen	Ich bringe dir die Einladung dann vorbei.	to bring sth. round

2

die 20er-Jahre-Party, -s	Wir möchten eine 20er-Jahre-Party feiern.	20s party

MODUL-PLUS AUSKLANG

1

✓ der Chauffeur, -e	Sie hat drei Autos und sogar einen Chauffeur.	chauffeur
✓ die Fantasie, Fantasien	Hast du denn wirklich keine Fantasie?	fantasy
✓ das Luxushaus, ⸚er	Sue wohnt in einem Luxushaus.	luxury house
✓ der Schmuck (Sg.)	Sie hat sehr teuren Schmuck.	jewellery

Lektion 22: Am besten sind seine Schuhe!

Degrees of adjectives and adverbs

The adjectives and some adverbs (e.g. gern or viel) have three degrees: **positive**, **comparative** and **superlative**. The positive is the basic form of the adjective or adverb. The comparative and the superlative forms will vary – depending on their regularity.

	regular adjective	regular adjective with added Umlaut	irregular adjective
positive	**schön**	**groß**	**gut**
comparative	**schön**er	**größ**er	besser
superlative	am **schön**sten	am **größ**ten	am besten

There is no rule, how the irregular adjective or adverb will change. It has to be memorized.

Ich trage **gern** Rosa.
Maria trägt noch **lieber** Rosa.
Anke trägt Rosa **am liebsten.**

I like wearing pink.
Maria likes wearing pink even more.
Anke likes wearing pink the most.

In German, the multi-syllable adjectives follow the same rules as the short ones. There is no more or most needed, e.g.:

langweilig (boring) → langweiliger → am langweiligsten

Comparison with wie and als

The prepositions **wie** and **als** are used to compare two things and express either equality or inequality.

or   so ...... wie

Equality: **genauso ... wie ...** (as... as...) + positive degree of adjective

Das T-Shirt ist **genauso** hässlich **wie** die Hose!   *The t-shirt is exactly as ugly as the trousers!*

Inequality: **als** (...than...) + comparative degree of adjective

Das T-Shirt ist sogar hässlicher **als** die Hose!   *The t-shirt is even more ugly than the trousers!*

Intensifying the statement

Some words used with right intonation can intensify the statement:

Das ist **lustig**!
Das ist **richtig** lustig!
Das ist **total** lustig!
Das ist **wahnsinnig** lustig!

It's funny!
*It's **really** funny!*
*It's **totally** funny!*
*It's **hilarious**!*

Grammar Explanations

Lektion 23: Ins Wasser gefallen?

Impersonal forms in weather descriptions

The impersonal pronoun **es** is used to describe the weather. It is followed by a conjugated verb or by the verb **sein** and an adjective.

Es schneit.	*It's snowing.*
Es regnet.	*It's raining.*

Es ist sonnig.	*It's sunny.*
Es ist windig.	*It's windy.*

In some cases there might be a noun in weather descriptions as well, e.g.:
Die Sonne scheint.   *The sun is shining.*

Cardinal directions

All names of the cardinal directions in German, are **masculine**:

der Norden	*the north*
der Westen	*the west*
der Süden	*the south*
der Osten	*the east*

The geographical names with cardinal directions don't have the ending **-en** and are written **together**:

Südtirol	*South Tyrol*
Ostdeutschland	*East Germany*
Nordamerika	*North America*

Word forming with -los

The ending **-los** can be added to a noun to form an adjective (sometimes there might be some adjustments necessary to the noun). The meaning of **-los** is the same as **-less** in English. It can be explained as *"without the noun"*

die Farbe + los → **farblos**
colour + less → **colourless**

die Wolke + los → **wolkenlos**
cloud + less → **cloudless**

Der Himmel ist heute **wolkenlos**.   *The sky is **cloudless** today.*

Clauses with denn

Denn (*because*) is a coordinating conjunction, connecting two "independent" clauses. The word order stays the same as if both sentences would be separate.

Es war perfekt, **denn** wir hatten ein Traumwetter	It was perfect, **because** we had a dream weather.

Lektion 24: Ich würde am liebsten jeden Tag feiern.

Subjunctive

Konjunktiv II, in English *subjunctive*, is a mood (not a tense!) used to express **hypothesis**, things that are **not a fact** and things that we would wish to become real. One of the subjunctive forms is „Ich möchte..."

The most common used form of subjunctive is **würde** (*would*), as an auxiliary with an **infinitive** of another verb.

Ich **würde** gern zu seiner Party **gehen**.	I **would go** to his party with pleasure.
Er **würde** am liebsten nach Las Vegas **fahren**.	He **would** like **to go** to Las Vegas the most.

All degrees of **gern** (gern → lieber → am liebsten) can be used in the sentences expressing our **wishes**.

		würde
singular	ich	**würde**
	du	**würdest**
	er/sie	**würde**
plural	wir	würden
	ihr	würdet
	sie/Sie	würden

The first and the third person singular of **würde** are identical.

Ordinal numbers

Ordinal numbers are formed from cardinal numbers: from **1** to **19** by adding the ending **-te** and from **20** and above **-ste**. 1st, 3rd, 7th and 8th are irregular.

<u>1 – 19 + -te</u>

1. erste	6. sechste	11. elfte
2. zweite	7. siebte	12. zwölfte
3. dritte	8. achte	13. dreizehnte
4. vierte	9. neunte	14. vierzehnte
5. fünfte	10. zehnte	15. fünfzehnte ...

Grammar Explanations

20 and above + -ste

20. zwanzigste
21. einundzwanzigste
30. dreißigste

Ordinal numbers can be shortened by adding a dot:

1. = 1st
2. = 2nd
3. = 3rd

Ordinal numbers can have the function of an adjective. They take the article of the noun:

der erste Januar   *the first of January*
die zweite Klasse   *the second class*
das dritte Kind   *the third child*

The ending of the ordinal number might change to **-ten** or **-sten** if the noun is used in a different case than nominative.

Wann hast du Geburtstag? **Am achten** Januar.   *When is your birthday? On the eighth of January.*

Wann bist du im Urlaub? **Vom ersten bis zum vierzehnten** August.   *When are you on holidays? From the first till the fourteenth of August.*

Customs, Festivals and Public Holidays in German Speaking Areas

Advent, the time of year between 1ˢᵗ and 24ᵗʰ of December, and the Christmas festivities themselves are of great importance in German speaking areas. Many traditions held by people all over the world have their origin in Germany and since *Advent* is also the time for home-baking, treats like *Christstollen, Spekulatius, Zimtsterne* and *Glühwein* are now well-loved delicacies beyond the German speaking areas.

Advent, Advent,

ein Kerzlein brennt!

Erst eins, dann zwei, dann drei, dann vier,

dann steht das Christkind vor der Tür.

The advent wreath (*Adventskranz*) is thought to be invented in the north of Germany in the 19ᵗʰ century and enjoys popularity in many countries world-wide. However, there is evidence from pre-Christian times that people lit candles on a wreath in the cold, dark months of the year and it has been tradition in Scandinavia for many centuries to light candles in winter to bring hope and warmth. Therefore, the actual origin of the advent wreath may be much older than previously assumed. The four candles represent the four weeks of *Advent.* One candle is lit in the first week, then an additional candle each week.

In many German speaking regions, the *Adventzeit* is ushered in with the opening of the *Weihnachtsmarkt,* in some areas also known as *Christkindlmarkt,* the street markets famous for delicious food, drinks and traditional hand-crafted products. The origin of Christmas markets goes back more than 600 years when traders and craftsmen were first given an opportunity to sell their home-made goods in the local market place. Through the years, Christmas markets became significant events as they were both a good opportunity to buy the necessities to get people through the dark season as well as to provide a welcome change during those long cold winter months.

One of the highlights for children during the advent season is the 6ᵗʰ of December -Nikolaustag (St. Nicholas day). The historic figure of Saint Nicholas is a fourth-century Greek bishop and Christian saint, known for his kindness to children and the giving of gifts.

Cultural Studies

On the night of the 5th of December, children leave their boots outside or by the fireplace and if they have been well-behaved *Nikolaus*, after consulting his golden book, awards them with little treats such as mandarins, nuts and sweets. In appearance, *Nikolaus* is similar to Father Christmas and Santa Claus wearing a thick red coat, a white beard and heavy black boots.

St. Nicholas traditions vary widely from region to region as does his name. The Swiss version of *Nikolaus* is called *Samichlaus* and his helper is known as *Schmutzli* referring to his dark clothes or his blacked out face. *Schmutzli* usually carries a bunch of twigs to punish children who hadn't behaved well throughout the year. In Germany and Austria, *Nikolaus* has different companions too, depending on the region you are in. His most famous companion is called *Knecht Ruprecht* (*Knecht* = servant) and according to the legend, he carries a big sack on his back for all the naughty children. Other likely assistants are St. Peter, an angel or the *Christkindl* (Christ child).

However, the scariest companions of *Nikolaus* have to be the devil-like *Krampus* creatures with their long horns, thick fur, pointed ears, huge cowbells and chains which are mainly featured in Austria, Bavaria and the German speaking area *Südtirol* (South Tyrol) in the north of Italy. The word *Krampus* originates from the Old High German word for

'claw' (*krampen*) and the figure itself shares many characteristics with other demonic individuals in Greek and Nordic mythologies. The beast-like creatures, which in some areas are also simply known as *Teufel* (devil), are said to emerge from their places in hell or the underworld on the 5th of December in order to dispense punishment on naughty children. Just like the Swiss counterpart *Schmutzli* and *Knecht Ruprecht*, they carry a bundle of sticks, a whip, a sack or a tub for the naughty little ones.

Nowadays, mainly in Alpine areas, the *Krampuslauf* (literally meaning *Krampus*-run) where hundreds of these devil-like creatures wander the streets looking for victims is a popular event with tourists and locals alike. Be aware though, due to their frightening presence, a *Krampuslauf* is certainly nothing for the faint-hearted.

Heiligabend (Christmas Eve), the main event for German speakers, takes place on the 24th of December and is traditionally a family affair. However, as we have learnt previously, family forms and structures have altered dramatically in the past few years and big family gatherings and huge feasts are becoming less common. The 25th and the 26th of December are public holidays and again mostly celebrated surrounded by close family and friends. The Christmas tree, or *Weihnachtsbaum* in German, is another custom developed in Germany that gained popularity outside of the country in or around the late 19th century.

The change of the year, in German known as *Silvester* due to the fact that the 31st of December is St. Sylvester's day (New Year's Eve), is another important festivity around this time of the year and is commonly spent with friends and family. Fireworks, parties, nice food and toasts at midnight are the main events and naturally, sparkling wine features prominently at all the festivities too.

The Easter celebrations, known in German as *Ostern*, officially last for two days (*Ostersonntag*, *Ostermontag*) even though many people take a few more days off and often enjoy a short holiday. *Osterhase* and *Ostereier* are two of the main customs that are still of enormous importance, especially for children. Tradition says the Easter bunny hides the painted Easter eggs and chocolate eggs in the garden and on Easter Sunday children go outside and look for them.

Pentecost, or *Pfingsten* in German, takes place on *Pfingstsonntag* and *Pfingstmontag* and both days are also public holidays in German speaking areas.

Quellenverzeichnis

Cover: © Getty Images/Pando Hall

Seite 4: Hand © fotolia/Aaron Amat
Seite 20: © PantherMedia/Carsten Butz
Seite 21: © fotolia/Vladislav Gajic
Seite 22: Turm © Thinkstock/iStock/Bertl123; Zürich © fotolia/gipfelstuermer
Seite 23: © Thinkstock/Comstock
Seite 24: Wecker © fotolia/ketrin; Fernseher © fotolia/Franz Pfluegl
Seite 31: © iStockphoto/kentarcajuan
Seite 39: © PantherMedia/asray Laleike
Seite 40: oben © Thinkstock/iStock/BasieB; unten © Hauptverband
    der österr. Sozialversicherungsträger, Wien
Seite 41: © DIGITALstock/F. Aumüller
Seite 58: © Thinkstock/iStock/LianeM
Seite 60: © fotolia/Martina Berg
Seite 61: © Florian Bachmeier, Schliersee
Seite 64: © fotolia/Dirk Schumann
Seite 72: © fotolia/Dirk Schumann
Seite 75: Advent © iStockphoto/mikebause; Weihnachtsmarkt © Thinkstock/iStockphoto
Seite 76: Nikolaus © iStockphoto/Embosser; Krampus © iStock/xochicalco
Seite 77: Ostereier © iStockphoto/aloha_17

Bildredaktion: Iciar Caso, Hueber Verlag, München